A Coward's Progress

by

St. John Barrett

PublishAmerica
Baltimore

ISBN: 1-4241-5511-8
PUBLISHED BY PUBLISHAMERICA, LLLP
www.publishamerica.com
Baltimore

Printed in the United States of America

To
My Lovely
and Beloved Wife,
Elisabeth Fuchs Barrett

A Coward's Progress

1

William Townsend and his grandson walked toward the entrance of the playground hand in hand. They separated at the gate. William entered through a freely spinning turnstile, while little Hugh went through an entrance tended by a neighborhood matron who looked at the tag suspended around his neck and recorded in her log his name and time of entry. His tag, edged in red, reflected that to play in the park he must be accompanied by an "adult" twelve years or older who would closely "supervise" him at all times.

Hugh's size did not match his age. But he made up in energy what he lacked in height and bulk. He did not walk; he ran, except when obliged to hold the hand of an adult. He blissfully ignored the multitude of bruises and abrasions his compact body always carried.

As soon and William and Hugh were inside the playground, Hugh ran to the slides and took his place behind three or four other children waiting to mount. Townsend reached the area a few seconds later and firmly planted himself on a bench, his cane clutched in both hands in front of him.

When it came Hugh's turn to mount, William rose and walked to the side of the slide. When Hugh reached the top of the slide, he looked down at his grandfather, waved, and smiled. Then he jumped—not onto the sliding surface, but over the side toward his grandfather, a few feet below. "Here I come!" William, startled, dropped his cane, held out his arms, and caught Hugh as he reached the ground.

"That was more fun than sliding down! Let's do it again!"

William gently lowered Hugh to the ground, no hair of his curly blond head displaced.

"No. We will not do it again. We shouldn't have done it this time.

Do you realize you could have knocked me down and broken my back again? I won't bring you to the park any more unless you promise not to do risky things."

Hugh's enormous blue eyes looked directly into William's. "I promise. Now let's go over to the swings."

* * *

William Townsend's episode with Hugh in the playground stirred one of his earliest memories. He was himself about Hugh's present age when his mother took him to a school playground in their hometown. After some time on the teeter-totter, his mother took him to the slides and left him in the line of children waiting to ascend the steps and slide down. When it came his turn, he suddenly panicked. He ran to his mother, sitting on a nearby bench, and buried his head in her lap.

"Look at the other children sliding down. Some are even smaller than you. Go ahead. Give it a try. I'll hold your hand while you go up the steps."

His mother lifted him to the ground and held his hand as they walked back to the slide. When, trembling, he reached the top of the steps, she let go his hand. He looked down at her while other children waited.

"Go ahead. You can do it. Just sit down and hold on to both sides. That's it. Now slide forward. You've got it! Let your hands slip down, but don't go too fast. There you are!"

Halfway down, William let go the sides and slid free the rest of the way. At the bottom, he grinned broadly and ran to his mother.

"I did it!" From that day, William loved to slide.

2

Being with Hugh stirred other memories from William's past. One Christmas, William's parents gave him a shiny red tricycle. He refused to ride. He knew that if he sat in the seat and put his feet on the pedals, the tricycle would spin out of control. No urging by his parents could countervail. Finally his mother picked him up, spanked him, put him sobbing on the seat, and with her hands on the handle bars pushed him gently forward. The pedals revolved, carrying his feet with them. Soon he was pushing on them, propelling himself. He happily pedaled everywhere.

And riding horseback. William contrived all means he could to avoid riding lessons, but eventually his not-inconsiderable pride forced him to try it with a group of students his own age. His timidity was gradually replaced by genuine pleasure in riding and a love for horses.

What else? Fear of heights. He had a school friend who, unlike himself, was totally unafraid of physical risk. The two of them occasionally played around railroad switch yards not far from William's home. The yards had a large water tower with a fixed ladder that did not reach the ground. The friend prevailed on William to boost him up to reach the ladder. The friend then mounted to reach the unprotected walkway that ran around the tank. Watching, William's blood ran cold.

William's fear of height was mitigated in at least one regard. The Townsends had two large cherry trees in their yard, a black tartaron and a Mary Ann, and William liked cherries. When in season, he would pick as many as he could while standing on the ground. When he had picked all within reach, he would step into the first crotch of the tree and pick more. With his attention focused on what was above rather than below, he found himself step-by-step ascending the tree. While this largely mitigated his fear of heights in climbing trees, he was to learn that it did not cure his fear of heights in other contexts.

While William was enrolled in high school drama class, his teacher took the class on a tour of the school stage. On the tour, the students climbed a fixed ladder to the scaffolding above the stage to observe the controls for the curtains and the lighting. William hung back while the others ascended. Finally, with the others almost out of sight, he took his first trembling step. He managed to the top of the ladder and, out of the sight of his classmates, managed to crawl across the scaffolding and down the other side.

William had one trivial pre-teen experience that seemed unconnected to anything else, but which years later became a matter for reflection. William was in the breakfast room of his family home at the same time as his sister, four years older, and a girl friend of hers. William was wearing kiddie blue-jeans held up by an elastic band. His hands were in his pockets. For no reason he was aware, William pushed down with both hands and his jeans slipped down, exposing his underwear. His sister immediately called out to his mother in the next room.

William's mother came in, quickly took in the scene, took William by one arm, and lead him to the hall powder room. Mother took down William's underpants and administered a solid spank to his bare bottom.

"Don't ever do that again!" William went sobbing to his room.

* * *

William had another experience in grade school, which he *did* know at the time was a watershed. One day on the second grade play area, William fell into playful wrestling with an older classmate. To his surprise, William proved the stronger of the two. His ability to take the other down stuck in his memory. A couple of years later, while William was enrolled in "opportunity class," a program permitting superior students to complete a full year's work in a single semester, he was shooting basketballs with a group of fourth graders on the court assigned to the fourth grade. The boy he had bested at wrestling two years earlier, called "Red," was among the fourth graders on the court.

William and Red went for the same rebound. Although a year younger than Red and painfully skinny, William was taller and quicker on the court. He reached over Red's outstretched hands, cleanly grabbed the ball, and hung a hook shot through the basket. William grinned smugly at Red. Red responded.

"You're not supposed to be on this court. This is for the fourth grade."

"I'm in opportunity class. I can play on any court I want."

"You can't play on this court. And if you don't get off, I'll put you off."

"Try! Remember when I put you down in second grade?"

By now William was advancing on Red with clenched fists. He swung wildly. Red neatly avoided the blow and countered with a hard right to the chin. William went down. As William struggled to rise, Red picked up a bucket of water used on the court to settle the dust and poured it over William's head. Red was grinning. The other boys were laughing. As the school bell rang ending recess, Red stood over William.

"Do you want to finish this later?"

"Sure. I can borrow my sister's bike and be back here at 4:00."

When William got home, he found his mother in the sun room. His sister was not yet home from junior high.

"I need to borrow Sis's bike."

"What for?"

"I got in a fight at school today and have to go back to finish it."

In his mind's eye, William could still see his mother on that day. He had come into the room just as she was just leaving. When he spoke, she stopped and turned to him. She put her hand to her forehead, taking several seconds before responding.

"I can't let you go. You know what the doctor says about over-exerting. I just can't let you go."

That was that. William had known full well what his mother's response would be. And it was what he wanted. The fear that had engulfed him since leaving the school yard dissolved. It was replaced by a new fear—the fear of returning to school the next day.

Next day, William sought out Red.

"My sister wouldn't let me borrow her bike." Red said nothing.

Some weeks later, while William was walking to the home of his music teacher for a scheduled piano lesson, he saw Red a block or so away walking toward him on the same side of the street. William turned off on a cross street and dawdled until Red had gone by. Although his emotions were not yet fully defined, he knew he was on a path to cowardice and deceit. He felt a knot of fear in his stomach.

3

Although his life outwardly seemed to go along pretty much the same, William became deeply unhappy with what he sensed to be a fall from grace. He made some adjustments.

One day on the school yard at junior high school, William and a classmate named George, who was a "somewhat" friend of William but also somewhat of a schoolyard bully, were exchanging playful punches when George's eyes hardened and he started throwing serious blows. When William protested, George asked, "Do you want to finish this tomorrow?" William said he would, and they agreed to meet.

That evening, William decided to bring up during dinner the matter of his projected fight. His sister was out for the evening, but both his parents were at the table, as was Mr. Parducci, a client his father had invited for the evening. Parducci, who sat opposite William, was the operator of a local winery. He was short and portly with a florid face and a nose displaying a multitude of small blue veins. As the cook cleared the salad plates, Mr. Parducci asked William how school had gone that day.

"Fine. But I got into kind of a fight during recess and we're supposed to finish it up tomorrow."

William's mother interjected, "What was the fight about?"

"Not really about anything. We were just horsing around—sparring—when he started hitting real hard. When I asked him to stop, he asked if I wanted to finish it tomorrow, and I said sure. So we agreed to meet tomorrow."

"Who was it?"

William said it was George, the son of parents that both of his own parents knew well.

"You know you're not allowed to fight. You'll just have to tell

13

George tomorrow that you've been ill and that your doctors don't allow fighting. What do you think, Mr. Parducci?"

Parducci put down his napkin and looked across at William. William knew a couple of Parducci's sons. They were part of a group of boys generally regarded by the other students as "tough."

"I think your mother is right. You will have to tell George that you can't fight."

Next day, William sought out George and told him what the adults had said he should say. But unlike with Red two or three years before, William did not avoid George. Indeed, he regularly sought him out, and they began doing small things together. Eventually, they appeared outwardly as school friends, and by time they were in high school George was picking up William in his Model A Ford in the morning and giving him a ride to school in the rumble seat.

While George seemed to have forgotten their earlier altercation, William had not. William knew that from his side the friendship was false.

4

While a teenager, William had a brush with religion but it didn't catch hold. His father came from a fundamentalist Baptist family and his mother form a conservative Methodist household. After marriage, they both found the Episcopal church more congenial in their particular social milieu. Although they did not keep alcohol in their home, his father was not averse to a social drink when they were out, and they both played bridge and danced. His father, who was a well-trained vocalist, joined the choir and was soon a principal soloist. Eventually, he assumed the office of Senior Warden, the principal lay office in the church, and later became chancellor of the diocese. Unsurprisingly, William's parents offered his services as an acolyte.

William was enrolled by his parents in a class for instruction in anticipation of confirmation into full church membership. He completed the course and was scheduled for confirmation with his class when the bishop next visited the church, but was ill at home when the day arrived. The bishop, a large man with a shock of white hair and portly bearing, offered to come to the Townsend home and, if William was agreeable, confirm him there. When the Bishop arrived from the church in full vestment, William was under a blanket on the sun room sofa. Asked by the bishop whether he wished to be confirmed, William replied, "You're the doctor. It's up to you." This bit of flippancy earned William a stern lecture after the bishop had left.

In any event, William said he would like to proceed, and the bishop began reading the service in his deep, sonorous voice. When he reached the point of the laying on of hands and praying that "this thy child" may "daily increase in thy Holy Spirit more and more," it came out in the bishop's stentorian tones as "mo-ah and mo-ah." William felt the

15

corners of his mouth. He knew that if he looked at his sister they would both be desperately suppressing giggles. They survived the moment, but long afterward would be saying "mo-ah," to their own endless delight and their parents' perplexity.

"I would like some mo-ah butter, please."

"But you are always asking for mo-ah and mo-ah."

The chief acolyte during William's period of service at the church was named Thomas and called Tommy by all. Tommy was a year or two older than William, was a handsome boy, good-natured, ever ready to smile, and a friend of all. Everyone loved Tommy. And, unlike William, he was a serious acolyte. He handled the items used in the communion service with sincere reverence. This was not apparent from anything he said, but from his care and gentle glow whenever he handled the chalice, the serving plate, the vials of wine or water, or the communion wafers. Although everyone was his friend, he never had a girl-friend. There was no doubt he was headed for a priestly career.

Tommy was the only child of near-destitute mite of a woman who sustained the two of them by doing house-work for church-members. She was herself a devoted church-member and a constant volunteer for church work within her competence. William was unaware of who or where Tommy's father was.

Years after William's service as an acolyte, he chanced to learn that Tommy's mother was working as a dish-washer in a restaurant where he was having lunch that day. He went to the kitchen to say hello and to offer his condolence for Tommy's death.

With financial support from the church, Tommy had enrolled on a scholarship at a seminary. While pursuing his studies he also served as a religious counselor at a nearby state penitentiary. One night, returning by foot to his seminary, he was struck and killed by a passing car. The driver reported to the police that Tommy, who was dressed in dark clothing and walking on the right side of the road, had stepped in front of his car, giving him no time to either brake or swerve. The driver was not charged. William, from first reading a news account, had wondered if Tommy had deliberately put himself at risk.

5

William had B-B guns when he was in grade school, and by time he entered junior high his parents had given him a single shot bolt-action .22 caliber rifle. Neither parent gave him any instruction on the care and use of fire-arms, but he learned willy-nilly through close family friends with whom he hunted or target practiced. In time, he fell heir to a couple of old double-barrel 12-gauge shotguns that had come down through the families of his two parents and a new 20-gauge Winchester pump that his father had somehow acquired but, to William's knowledge, had never used. It was the 20-gauge that seared itself into William's memory.

William had free rein to shoot rats around the family home and yard, and generally used his .22 for the job. One day, however, he decided to use the 20-gauge shotgun. He took the gun to the backyard with a box of shells, loaded the magazine, and pumped a shell into the chamber. Not having used the gun before, he was not altogether sure what position the safety button should be in to render the gun "safe." He put it in the position that he thought was "safe" and pressed the trigger to confirm his belief. The gun erupted. It kicked almost out of his grip and sent a charge of shot ricocheting off a flagstone about ten feet in front of him, leaving a smear of lead where it had struck. He ejected the spent casing, emptied the magazine, returned the unused shells to their box, and went back in the house. He carried the gun to his bedroom, cleaned the residue from inside the barrel, and replaced the gun in his closet. He then sat on the edge of his bed and began to weep.

His mother found him weeping. When she asked what was wrong, he told her what had happened.

"It's alright. Your just scared. You'll get over it." She didn't tell him how stupid he had been. She didn't say anything about using guns in the future. She simply left him sitting on the edge of the bed.

* * *

In running to his parents when he needed help to gain some or another end, William often shaded the truth in enlisting their help—or in avoiding their intrusion. One such occasion related to a favorite pastime—fishing.

William fished for large-mouth bass in the town reservoir with a junior college student who had been employed as gardener and handyman by his mother. William and Lawrence had become fast friends, and William had frequently gone hunting or fishing with Lawrence. Lawrence was small but wiry and completely fearless. He had a way of ingratiating himself with strangers and had gained, one way or another, the confidence and friendship of the caretaker at the town reservoir, a few miles outside the city limits. The reservoir was a spring-fed pool behind an earth dam, the inner surface of which was lined by quarried stone. Underwater, the fissures between the stones provided shelter for crappie, a small perch-like fish with a spiky dorsal. More importantly, in the deep water behind the dam groups of large-mouth black bass and calico bass would cruise the crystal water looking for anything edible, including crappie.

Lawrence and William would take to the reservoir a bucket, a can of worms, and hand lines with small bait hooks. Looking into the water from the top of the dam, they could see the noses of crappie peeking out from the rocks and, by dangling worms in front of the noses, would soon have a bucket of lively crappie to use as bait for the bass. They would then take to their casting rods, and cast a live crappie as far as they could into the reservoir. A soon as it hit the water, the crappie would head for the shelter of the rocks, and, if it crossed the path or came within the sight of a bass, it would almost surely be gobbled up. Then the fun began, ending with a bass swept into their landing net.

After Lawrence had left town to attend university, William would venture to fishing spots he had learned of from Lawrence, including the reservoir. One day, he bicycled with two buddies—brothers who lived in a house behind his own—to the reservoir with the usual fishing gear.

They by-passed the care-taker's cabin and set up their gear on the top of the dam. Two small boys—maybe five and seven—came out of the cabin and walked to them.

While the two boys watched them setting up to catch crappie, William opened a conversation with the older of the two

"How long you lived out here?"

"We came awhile back. After I finished school. I'm going to start in a new school this year."

"It must be great living out here. You can fish and swim all summer."

"We don't swim. It's not allowed."

"I'll bet you do. How can you live right next to it and not swim when other people aren't around?"

After watching a bit more, the boys wandered back to the cabin.

A few minutes later a man in overalls strode from the cabin toward William and his friends.

"What you boys doing here?"

"Fishing. We've been here before, and the watchman who lived here said it was O.K."

"Why you been asking my boys if they swam in the reservoir?"

William did not answer.

"You kids get out of here and don't come back."

William and his friends packed up their gear and left. When home, William told his father the new watchman had kicked them off the reservoir.

"Why wouldn't he let you fish?"

"He didn't say. No reason."

"Do you have any idea why he ordered you off?"

William paused. "No idea."

William's father suggested William go to the office of the water company and ask for written permission to fish. As William knew, his father was well-acquainted with the owners.

William went to the downtown office of the water company and readily obtained a letter stating that he and his friends had permission to fish.

William and his friends returned to the reservoir with their gear. They dismounted from their bicycles and went to the door of the cabin. William knocked. When the door opened, the caretaker stood looking down at them. William handed him the letter. He read it and tore it up.

"As long I work here, none of you are going to come on this property."

As the caretaker firmly closed the door, William could see the two small boys listening from inside.

William and his friends mounted their bikes and rode home. William's father was at home when he arrived.

"You didn't stay long. How was the fishing?"

"The caretaker wouldn't let us in."

"Did you show him the letter?"

"He tore it up and said we couldn't come on the reservoir as long as he worked there."

"We'd better go back and talk to him. There's something here I don't understand."William's father backed the family car out of the garage. His mother got in the passenger side of the front seat. They left one of the back doors open for William. He didn't get in.

"Come on, get in."

"I'm not going."

"Come on. We can't go without you."

"I'm not going."

William's mother got out of the car, and his father pulled it back into the garage. All three went back into the house. They never talked about the reservoir again.

6

As the reservoir incident had illustrated, William Townsend had not only an urgent fear of physical risk, but had developed and nursed fears that were purely social.

In grammar school, he was tall for his age but painfully skinny. He had large ears that protruded at right angles. His classmates called him " Dumbo," after a flying elephant in a popular Disney animation, or sometimes "Ichabod" after the gangly protagonist in a story by Washington Irving. When he came from school weeping, his mother would tell him that his classmates gave him nicknames because they liked him, and he should just laugh it off. Easier said than done.

His social disaffection was aggravated as a result of a serious case of meningitis he contracted while in grammar school. It left him with a tremor, particularly in his hands but also in other parts of his body when under stress.

His physical tremor became a major matter of concealment and evasion. He declined drinks served in cups on saucers or in stemmed glasses. He did his best to avoid participating in piano recitals and succeeded only when his mother had witnessed the disaster of his performance in the only one she compelled him to appear. He declined chemistry as an elective course in high school on the ground he "wasn't interested" in chemistry, when his real reason was fear of handling test tubes and beakers. In the fifth grade, he avoided writing with chalk on the blackboard in front of his classmates by excusing himself to go to the boys' toilet just before it came his turn to go to the blackboard.

On the other hand, his voice was always clear and firm. And his oral reading was expressive. Whenever a teacher wanted a volunteer to read aloud some or another book passage, William's classmates would push him to the fore. And he came to enjoy it. But he panicked at the suggestion of a public appearance. When his junior high English teacher designated him to recite *The Blue and the Grey* during the annual Memorial Day celebration in the town's Veterans' Park, he told his mother he had been asked to recite *Little Boy Blue* and implored her to get him out of it. She did.

There was one public appearance, however terrifying in prospect, he knew he could not avoid. Unsurprisingly, he was selected to serve as valedictorian at his high school graduation.

He knew there was too much prestige attached to the selection for his parents to permit him to decline. So, all he could do was prepare. He labored mightily, with faculty help, on the text of a speech. Then he labored mightily on delivery. He even recorded the speech at the local radio station for play-back. He memorized so throughly he could completely disconnect his brain from his performance and not miss a beat. Because the graduating class was the largest in the school's history, the ceremony was held in the town's largest movie theater rather than the school auditorium.

William stepped to the podium at graduation with a strange mix of seemingly overwhelming fear and of confidence. The speech went well. His voice was strong and he enunciated clearly. Nobody in the theater, he was later told, had any trouble hearing. He had oceans of compliments, both on the speech itself and on his appearance. He was pleased.

* * *

While the valedictorian at William's high school had always been a boy, a second student speaker, designated "salutatorian," had always been a girl. The parents of the salutatorian for William's class invited various of the class officers and participants in the commencement, together with their dates, to dinner at their home before the senior ball, which was to be held at the town country club. The dinner threatened a maximum stress occasion for William—with water goblets, cups and saucers, and who-knew-what-else in a formal setting. To provide himself the greatest possible psychological cushion, he rested the entire day before the party. As a result—as he might have expected—he was tight as a drum when it came time to go. But, declining all liquids, he managed to get through the dinner with no major disaster and at the dance, released from the tension, thoroughly enjoyed himself.

7

William's experience with girls during his public school years was fleeting. During his second stint in a grade school "opportunity" class he was assigned to sit at a small table opposite a girl named Frances, who was exceptionally well developed for her age. What he remembered her for, however, was her kindness. Whenever his writing hand trembled in front of her, she would smile warmly at him without saying a word. She seemed to exude sympathy.

When Frances and William were back with the regular class in the sixth grade, it happened that they were taken on a class outing to the municipal swimming pool next door to the school. William was deathly afraid of the water, but managed to splash around a bit in the shallow end. Otherwise, he sat at the side of the pool with a group of boys watching the other swimmers. One of those swimmers was Frances, who was sitting very handsomely at the other end of the pool next to the diving board. The boys' conversation centered on the possibility of diving under water when she got in so they could grope her under the water. William was revulsed.

In junior high school periodic dances were held in the gym as a part of the physical education program. Group instruction was given in social dancing and the social graces related to dancing.

"May I have the pleasure of this dance?"

"Thank you for the dance."

Attendance was compulsory, and students were expected to wear clothing suitable for a party. The girls wore dresses below knee length and the boys jackets and ties. Boys were lined up on one side of the gym, and girls on the other. On cue, the boys crossed the floor en-masse to ask individual girls for a dance. William always raced across to ask a particular girl whom he always remembered as wearing a blue taffeta party dress with puff sleeves. She had moved from Alaska with her family, and was called "Snowbound" by fellow students. William thought she was the cat's whiskers. She had light taffy hair cut in a bob and wore no cosmetics. She was very slender and not particularly athletic. She was not a top student, but appeared very serious in all she did. She was very quiet and never volunteered in class. William had no contact with her other than in dancing class. They had very little conversation when they danced.

During William's final semester in junior high school, a group of boys that he knew organized a party to be held in the loft of an old carriage house at the home of one of his friends. At an organizing meeting in the loft, they agreed on particular tasks to be performed in preparing for the party—selecting dance records, setting up the sound system, cleaning the loft, refreshments, decorations, and the like. Each boy was asked to indicate a girl that he would like invited, with the thought that written invitations would be sent and each boy would arrange transportation for the girl he had indicated. William declined indicating a girl, whereupon his friends said they would indicate Snowbound for him and he would have to arrange her transportation. William was surprised his crush on Snowbound had been so obvious. He had never been teased about it, nor had it even been mentioned by his classmates. Over his weak protest, they decided she would be invited with him in mind.

The party was a smashing success. William had had no alternative but to telephone Snowbound and offer her a ride. Inasmuch as William did not yet have his driver's license, William's parents drove the two teenagers in the family Buick. William and Snowbound sat at opposite ends of the back seat. William's parents chit-chatted a bit with Snowbound about school, about how she liked moving here from Alaska, and the like. In letting the two out, the Townsends said they would pick up the two teenagers at midnight, the planned end of the party.

At the party, William took some refreshments to Snowbound, but he did not dance with her after the first obligatory turn around the floor.

24

She had plenty of other partners. He did dance with other girls and with the mother of the boy at whose home the party was being held. Finally, when the last dance was announced, he returned to Snowbound.

"May I have the last dance?"

"Of course."

They danced in silence. When they had descended the ladder from the loft and returned to the street, the Townsend Buick was waiting. William helped Snowbound into the back seat, went around the car, and got into the opposite corner. Again his parents chit-chatted with Snowbound. When they reached Snowbound's home, William got out, helped Snowbound out, walked her to her front door, thanked her for attending the party with him, and left.

On the ride home William barely spoke.

"How was the party?"

"Fine."

"Did Dorothy seem to enjoy it?

"Yes."

"She seems a very nice girl."

"She is."

William's stomach was churning. He never spoke to Snowbound again.

8

While William was in high school there were two incidents that particularly exposed the depth of his alienation.

The first was an experience with his classmate and good friend Bill, one of three redheaded sons of a widowed mother. Bill was the youngest, the shortest, and the bounciest of the three—a friend of everyone, always smiling and joking, ever ready to engage in any mischief. He enrolled in the Royal Canadian Air Force before the United States entered the war, served as a fighter pilot, and was killed in the Battle of Britain—but that gets ahead of our story.

Bill was a year older than William, and therefore had his drivers license before William. He also had intermittent use of his mother's car, an old black box of a Studebaker.

Bill had been given responsibility—probably in some Future Farmers of America program—for tending a pregnant sow through her anticipated delivery in the summer. The sow, a huge brute with no qualities to engender affection, was boarded on a pig farm some distance from town. Bill enlisted William in the venture, and each day the two of them would bump and sway their way out to the farm in the old Studebaker to tend the sow, which they did not bother to name.

Finally, word came. The sow had commenced labor. Bill and William piled into the Studebaker to attend. When they arrived, she had already delivered one squealing piglet and in short order delivered eleven more. Then, by way of after-thought, she delivered a tiny, unattractive runt. The sow carefully licked each piglet, including the runt. While she lay on her side, the squealing piglets tumbled and shoved to get to her teats. William reached in with one foot to separate the runt from the others. Then he ground the head of the runt into the dirt with the heal of his shoe. Bill watched in horror.

"The runt always dies anyway. It has to be killed."

When the sow and her piglets were settled, Bill and William left in silence. While driving home, neither spoke. When Bill dropped off William, they each simply said, "Good night."

William had felt no emotion when he killed the piglet. It would be years before his underlying emotions sufficiently surfaced to be felt.

* * *

William's second particularly disturbing experience during high school was of a very different sort.

William's mother intermittently engaged Lawrence to take William on fishing trips outside the area of their hometown. One such trip was to the area of Lake Tahoe. After several days of camping out of their car and somewhat desultory fishing, Lawrence learned from some of the locals that the Rubicon River was yielding major catches of rainbow trout, but getting there would require a substantial hike and camping over. They decided to give it a try. Each had an army blanket, in which he rolled spare clothes, food, and gear. Slinging their bed-rolls over their shoulders, they set off. The trail was barely discernable by blaze marks on the trees. Their blanket-packs soon rotated so that the cord tying the ends together was cutting their shoulders. It was unseasonally warm, the trail steep, the footing difficult, and mosquitoes swarmed whenever they stopped. Their geologic survey maps, however, were excellent, and they did not get lost. William could not keep to Lawrence's pace and lagged behind. Lawrence frequently stopped to let William catch up.

"Do you want to stop and blow awhile?"

"Give me half a minute and I'm ready."

Finally, while on a downhill they heard the river's roar. As they descended it grew louder. When it burst into view between the trees, they stood before a torrent. It was unlike any fishing stream they had seen. They found a level spot, cut green boughs to sleep on that night, suspended their perishable food between two trees, and set up camp. After eating their first meal since breakfast, they assembled their fishing gear and walked to the river's edge. The river was a raging torrent, churning and frothing as it gushed over and around huge boulders. There was no way to fish that rampage. But when they looked directly down from their granite perch into a quiet backwater they could see in the crystal water swarms of trout in refuge from the torrent. They baited their hooks with live worms and dropped them down. They could see a trout immediately seize each worm. They caught eight pan-sized trout—all they could possibly eat that evening and in the morning—and returned to camp. While they lounged, resting from their morning exertion, they discussed returning next year. They would definitely come back, but at least a month later when the run-off from the winter snow was diminished.

Next year they came back as planned, better equipped and eager to tackle a more manageable stream. As they came down the final slope toward their last-year's campsite, there was no river roar. The silence was eerie. When they reached their campsite and sloughed off their packs, there was still no sound. They ran to the river bank. The river had essentially disappeared. There was a huge gorge of boulders with intermittent pools of clear water and water flowing under the boulders from one pool to the next. It should be good fishing, but very different from the previous year.

After setting up camp, Lawrence and William set to fishing. It was tough going. Getting from one pool to the next required climbing over or going around huge boulders. They caught few fish, and those they caught were small. As they usually did when fishing a stream, the two became separated. William, who lagged behind, kept thinking he would come within sight of Lawrence when he came around or over one of the boulders. But he couldn't sight Lawrence, even when he hurried to catch up. He began feeling very much alone. He called out. No answer. He had a vision of last year's gushing torrent that had engulfed the very rock on which he now stood. He lost interest in fishing. In fear, he began scrambling over the boulders—and running when he could—to rejoin Lawrence. He also continued calling out. Nothing but silence and an eerie emptiness. Finally, coming around a huge boulder he saw Lawrence, calmly fishing a placid pool. William's panic evaporated, and he resumed fishing. But he never forgot his underlying terror.

9

Being with Hugh continually evoked in William recollections of his past that had long been submerged. And it was also creating new memories.

A couple of years after the incident with Hugh at the slide, William was again taking Hugh to the playground. On entering they went to the swings. Hugh lined up behind several other children to await his turn. An older boy, Tom, joined the line behind Hugh. As Hugh stepped forward in the line one of his sneakers came off. Tom had given him a "flatsy" by stepping with the toe of his shoe on the heal of Hugh's sneaker.

"Don't do that!"

Tom looked steadily into Hugh's eyes, but said nothing. Hugh bent over and re-tied his sneaker just in time to take his turn on the next available swing. The swings were the old-fashion type—a well-worn board suspended by two hand-friendly ropes. As soon as Hugh grabbed the ropes and stepped onto the swing Tom, who had come up behind, grabbed the seat and started rotating it.

"Let go!"

Tom let go, but only after he had twisted the ropes tightly together. The board on which Hugh stood began slowly rotating and then picked up speed until—or so it felt to Hugh—it was going like an electric mixer. It then slowed and stopped only to rotate back in the other direction. Back and forth. When it finally wound down, Hugh slithered off and staggered to a nearby bench.

Tom, who had caught the swing to take his turn, looked over at Hugh.

"What a great swing! Too bad your supervisor couldn't see it."

Hugh, still feeling vertigo, jumped up and lunged at Tom with clenched fists.

Tom was ready for him. He neatly avoided Hugh's wild swing and planted a solid right to Hugh's cheek. Hugh went down. Tom stood over him. By then, a crowd of children had collected, and the playground monitors would soon follow.

"If you want to finish this, let's go down to the soccer field."

"I'll see you there."

Hugh found his grandfather on a bench a short distance away reading his newspaper. He appeared not to have seen what happened at the swings.

"I have to go down to the soccer field to finish a fight I got into at the swings."

"Oh? What was the fight about?"

"Tom kept bugging me when I tried to swing. He's bugged me before, and I've always ignored it."

"Can't you settle it without a fight?"

"Maybe. But I said I'd meet him on the soccer field."

"Then you'd better go. I'll walk down with you."

When they reached the field, there was already a group of children standing inside the gate.

"That's him. The big guy in the red sweater."

"O.K. I'll wait here while you go in."

All eyes turned to Hugh as he walked toward the group. While he was walking, the group re-formed itself in a circle with Tom in the center. Hugh entered the circle and stepped toward Tom.

"Who's that old geek standing by the fence."

"He's my grandfather. He's just watching."

Tom and Hugh started circling, feeling each other out. Hugh tried a couple of left jabs, which Tom easily blocked and countered with a hard right that caught Hugh on the eye.

William, leaning on the fence next to the gate, saw a middle-aged woman hurrying from the direction of the playground. She reached him somewhat out of breath.

"Do you know there's a fight going on down there?"

"Yes, I know."

"Who are they?"

"One of them's my grandson."

"Aren't you going to stop them?"

"They're doing alright. My kid's getting licked, but otherwise he's doing O.K."

"Well, I'm going to stop it!"

With that, she took off running to the group of children.

"Stop! Stop! We don't allow fighting anywhere in the park."

She looked at their tags and noted their names. "Both of you leave the park and don't come back until we've contacted your parents."

Hugh came back to William, and together they walked home. Once home, William told Hugh to wash up. Then he put a patch on Hugh's eye, which was turning black.

"Do you know where Tom lives?"

"No, but he lives somewhere in the neighborhood. I see him around on his bike."

"I'll find out from the playground people where he lives. I want to go with you to see Tom and his parents."

Later, William and Hugh approached a medium size split-level house several blocks away. A middle-age man sat at a table on the porch reading the sports section of the newspaper while drinking a mug of coffee. He wore an undershirt tucked into blue jeans and had tattoos on both shoulders. William mounted the porch and extended his hand.

"Hello. My name is William Townsend and this is my grandson Hugh. We live down on Tucker Street. Hugh and your son Tom got in a fight over in the playground this morning and we thought we'd come talk to you before the playground people came around."

"Tom! Come out here! We need to talk to you."

Tom came out the front door.

"This is Mr. Townsend. I guess you know Hugh. You didn't tell me you got in a fight in the playground this morning."

"It wasn't much of a fight. Mrs. Stevenson broke it up."

"Not much of a fight? What about Hugh's eye?"

"It was just a lucky shot. I wasn't trying to hit hard."

"What were you fighting about?"

"Not much. He thought I was bugging him. But everybody's always bugging everyone else on the playground. Maybe he's sensitive."

"Is there any reason you two can't agree to leave each other alone?"

"I guess not. If he'll agree, I'll agree."

Tom held out his hand, and Hugh took it. Hugh and William left. They had said nothing after the initial introductions.

Walking home, William felt a little light headed, as though a great burden had been lifted from him. It had been a small matter, easily resolved, but his heart sang inexplicably. It struck him it may have been a redemptive event.

10

There was another event during William's high school years that he did not much note at the time, but later became a matter for reflection.

William had intermittent bouts of hay fever starting in grade school. He sneezed loudly and, once started, it seemed he would go without end. By-and-large, this posed no problem until in high school he was enrolled in study hall. Study hall was in a large room with eighty or a hundred desks secured to the floor in four rows. A tiny lady, wearing rimless glasses and with white hair tied in a bun, presided over students from all grades who were assigned to the hall to do whatever homework they might have, and otherwise read, draw or whatever. Mrs. Smith had been rehired to perform this seemingly simple role after retiring as an English teacher. All she had to do was take roll and maintain order. She did the latter with a vengeance. Once "class" was convened, one could have heard a pin drop. How such a tiny, white-haired spinster could so terrorize a bunch of otherwise rambunctious teenagers was one of life's mysteries.

William was assigned a desk about half-way back in the row nearest the windows. One day he started sneezing. The first sneeze brought no particular notice, but as they continued the eagle eye of Mrs. Smith locked on to William. At the sixth sneeze, she picked up her ruler, rose slowly to her feet, and began to move on little cat's feet toward William's bowed head. Her gaze did not deviate. Nobody looked up.

William felt another tingling at the bridge of his nose.

"Aaaah choo!"

"I can't help it. I have hay fever."

"Go out in the hallway. I will see you in the principal's office at 3:30."

There wasn't a sound, but all eyes were on William as he walked to the door and went into the hallway.

At 3:30, William was seated across from the principal, with Mrs. Smith seated primly to the side.

"I can't help it. Once I sneeze, my hay fever won't let me stop."

"Sneeze all you want, but don't do it any more in study hall."

"Yes, sir."

To William's surprise, he never sneezed again in study hall, although he was by no means cured of sneezing elsewhere.

* * *

William developed a couple of other physical quirks during his secondary school years that provided grist for reflection in his later years. One was a tendency to migraine headaches. The headaches were infrequent and seemed unconnected to any event in his life, but when they came they were severe. They would start at the back of his brain, first at low intensity and then building to throbbing, searing pain. If he was lying down, it would be almost impossible to get up. By time he was through high school, however, he was free of them.

The other quirk was not really all that quirky. William and his two friends who lived in the house behind his own had become acquainted with the son of a recently arrived English couple who moved in a block away. The English boy, whom we shall call "Henry," was a bit older, a bit taller, considerably more agile, and smarter than William and his two friends. He also had a wonderful assortment of toys that he had brought from England—an electric train set, an erector set, toy soldiers, bows and arrows, costumes—and had a large play-room in his home in which he and his friends had free reign. The upshot was he became not only a neighborhood buddy, but a leader.

Henry was also a compulsive finger-biter. The skin around his fingernails was raw. And William began biting. When William's mother noted his new habit, she readily made the connection with the condition of Henry's fingers. She told William if he didn't stop biting she would forbid his further seeing Henry. William didn't stop, but she never imposed the interdiction.

William himself, even as early as high school, came to view finger-

34

biting as a stupid habit, and he vowed to stop it. But he couldn't. It was only much later in life he grasped the connection between his biting and his inner stress. An incipient bite, suspended in mid-air, could then lead him to an inner feeling to be dealt with.

11

William's infatuation with Snowbound did not survive his escorting her to the dance in the carriage loft. Nor was it replaced by another similar attraction. He did, however, attend social occasions, including school dances, that called for him to escort a date, and he developed somewhat jocular social relations with a series of girls. One of these was Patricia.

Patricia was about a year younger than William and lived with her parents and younger brother about two blocks from the Townsends. She was a pretty girl, taller than average, with light taffy colored hair, regular features, and clear peaches-and-cream complection. Although not an exceptional student, she was bright and playful, as were her parents. William joked back and forth with the three of them, and they soon became neighborhood friends. More than that, they all enjoyed playing various games, and William was soon playing Chinese checkers, Scrabble, Monopoly, bridge, poker, ping pong and other games at their house.

One afternoon Pat called William and suggested that he come over that evening while here parents were at a party. Pat's brother would be out with friends. William readily agreed and arrived after her parents had left. When she opened the door for him, she was wearing a full length dressing gown with a zipper down the front. William presumed she was wearing her nightgown underneath.

"My folks asked that I say hello for them. Dad said they would call home fifteen minutes before they left the party. I've set up the games in the study."

Stepping into the study, William saw the Scrabble board resting on the center cushion of the sofa and the other games and game boards resting on a card table.

"O.K., so we start with scrabble."

William and Pat were both mean scrabblers. They often challenged each other's words and imposed a three point penalty for each unsuccessful challenge. Webster's Unabridged lay on the window ledge as the ultimate arbiter.

"Ur isn't a word. I challenge."

"Of course it is. It was an ancient city somewhere around the Fertile Crescent. It appears in the Bible."

"We're not supposed to use words and names appearing only in the Bible. We're in penalty land."

"No, we aren't. I'll show it to you."

William rose and went to the window ledge. Pat followed. He began riffling the pages at "un," his right hand running down the page as he drew close. Her hand followed his.

"Here it is. Just like I said." Pat placed her hand lightly on the back of William's as she looked at the entry.

"O.K., I'll give you the penalty, but I wonder about this Webster guy. Next time I'm going to have an Oxford Unabridged."

They left "ur" on the board and William promptly tacked on the seven letter word "unquiet."

Shortly before midnight, Pat's Dad called to say they would be leaving the party within the next ten minutes. Pat promptly put the games away even though she urged William to stay until her parents arrived.

"Why don't you wait 'til they come? They always take longer than they say."

"No, I'm going."

William went to the front door, opened it, and stepped outside. Facing Pat, he said "Goodnight. Thanks for the games."

"Goodnight. You're welcome." She smiled faintly

William turned on his heel and walked home. He had a vague feeling he had somehow let Pat down.

* * *

Sometime after William's evening with Pat in her home, he invited her to go with him to an informal get-together at a friend's home. There were refreshments and games and a bit of dancing to recorded music. One of the other guests was a freshly minted navy sailor who came without a date. At one point in the evening some of the other guests called William's attention to the fact that Pat and the sailor had disappeared from the party. A half-hour later Pat re-appeared and then, after another five minutes, the sailor re-appeared. Pat offered no explanation for her absence. William didn't ask.

12

One of William's best friends in junior high school was Jim. Their families were also friends—their mothers members of the same bridge club, their families members of the same church, and William's father and Jim's mother singers in the same choir. Both mothers had served as elementary school teachers and both still served as substitute teachers. Both boys were good students, not particularly athletic, and each was enrolled a year ahead of his age level. And the families were congenial—having largely the same interests and enjoying the same jokes.

Jim and William both played card games, sometimes for small sums of money. One afternoon after school they were playing at the home of a mutual friend, when they got in an argument over whether Jim had stayed in or dropped out of a particular poker pot that William had won.

"You know you stayed in. You certainly didn't say you were dropping out."

"I didn't put another dime in to stay."

"But you made a gesture as though you were staying. If you had won the pot, don't tell me you wouldn't have claimed it. You owe me a dime."

"I don't owe you anything."

William reached out and pushed Jim back in his chair. His head went back and struck the headrest. Jim got up, put on his sweater, and left the house.

William felt good about his performance. He had challenged Jim and Jim had backed off.

William and Jim had no contact until a month or so later Jim was riding in a car driven by another classmate when it stopped at William's home. William went out to the car just as Jim stepped out the left rear door. Jim looked over the top of the car directly at William.

"Hello, William."

William was surprised—first, because he was expecting some diffidence from Jim by reason of their earlier encounter, and, second, because Jim had never before addressed him by his full first name.

"Hello, Jim."

For the rest of their lives, Jim addressed William by his full first name. All other classmates and friends addressed him as "Bill." William knew that Jim was sending him a constant message. And it soon became a message of constant torment.

With time's passage, William's friendship with Jim was restored and even strengthened, but neither of them ever spoke of the altercation in the poker game.

13

When it came time for college, William simply followed the path of least resistance. He enrolled in a small, but prestigious, liberal arts college his sister was attending. He was scared to death but was resolved to do well. And he did. He got straight A's in his academic subjects plus being awarded the yearly freshman English prize and a competitive scholarship. And he was well-liked. But his tremor stayed with him, as did his self-protective maneuvers. After failing some written examinations because he could not write fast enough, he arranged to take written essay exams on a typewriter. Socially, he avoided afternoon teas.

When William's freshman English class was assigned a topic on which each student was to write something—an essay, a story, some poetry, or whatever—William tried to dredge from his deepest consciousness. And he gained praise from both his instructor and his classmates when his instructor read in class bits and pieces from his papers. But there was one of his papers from which his instructor did not read in class. William did not know it at the time, but the topic was derived from his feelings when he had killed the piglet. It had to do with tension, rage, and violence. Nothing warm and fuzzy. William's instructor raised it with him in a private conference. The instructor said it "frightened" him. Although William saved his other English papers, this one he destroyed.

Thanksgiving recess his sophomore year brought an event that would alter his life course. He was seated alone in the breakfast room at home over breakfast when he felt a tingling in the tip of his tongue. He started falling to his left, unable to stop himself. Halfway to the floor, he lost consciousness. When he came to, he was lying on the couch in the sun room with their family physician looking down. He was told he had had some sort of convulsion and would be taken to the hospital. After a brief stay in the local hospital, his father drove the entire family to the University Hospital, some sixty miles away, where William was to undergo various tests and be examined by the Chief of Neurology.

When William's father pulled the family Buick to the front of the hospital, William was sitting on the edge of his seat. His father had always had a deep aversion to any medical procedures, and William was tight as a spring to see how he would perform now.

"Go on in with Mother."

"Aren't you coming in?"

"Get out of the car!"

William got out of the car and went in with his mother.

Seated in the lobby, William's mother explained to him what he already knew.

"Your father really didn't mean to speak that sharply to you. You know how he has always been unable to deal with medical situations." Indeed, William remembered how his father had to excuse himself from the movie *Birth of a Baby* which the family was attending at the World's Fair and how he repeatedly postponed visiting seriously ill clients and ended up not visiting them at all. But surely he should have shared with his son a visit to a brain surgeon about a possibly life-threatening condition. But, as usual, it was his mother who took the oars.

William's stay in the hospital revealed that the root of his problem was some scar tissue left at the base of his brain by the same childhood illness that had left him with his tremor. He was put on a mild dosage of phenobarbital and was directed to strictly limit his liquid intake and somewhat limit his physical activities. His drivers license was suspended until further notice.

With the end of Thanksgiving recess, William returned to college no worse for wear and resumed his former activities—indeed, he may even have pushed them up a notch. He played inter-fraternity basketball with no less endurance and much sharper focus than before.

William had been working out with the college basketball team, although he was not a team member. He had been only a mildly good shot and was awkward on the floor. But when he returned to school after his epileptic seizure, he found he performed better than ever. On one occasion, after wind sprints, William and the players he worked out with were taking practice free shots, something William had been only moderately good at. Now he was perfect. The universal style of free throw shooting at that time was under-handed with both hands. William stood at the line completely relaxed, his eyes firmly focused on the front rim. With both arms at full extension, he would propel the ball delicately on his finger-tips. Swoosh! Nothing but net. Ten for ten. William was confident he could have swooshed a hundred for a hundred.

Also, in scrimmage he was more alert. In inter-fraternity basketball he played center by reason of his height and long arms. In its last and crucial game William was the first of his team to confront their opponents as they came down the floor on each new possession. William would have his eyes locked on the man dribbling the ball. He knew exactly what point in his opponent's dribble he was within reach. At that point, the instant the ball descended from his opponent's hand, William would dart. He never missed. Nor did his opposing center learn. This was an experience that William would never repeat.

On December 7 Japan attacked Pearl Harbor, and the United States entered the war in both Europe and the Pacific. William registered for the draft. In the meantime, his mother obtained a for-whom-it-may-concern letter from his neurosurgeon and instructed him to present it to his draft board when he reported for his physical. The letter said that he had suffered a *grande mal* epileptic seizure by reason of scar tissue at the base of his brain that somehow inter-played with a psychosomatic syndrome. He presented the letter to his draft board and was duly classified 4F—physically unfit for service.

William graduated on an accelerated schedule, and went home to wait out the war. While home, three of his fraternity brothers went out of their way to visit him before shipping out. It oppressed him that they were going and he was staying, and he wondered if he shouldn't have simply torn up the letter from the neurologist that his mother had provided for his draft board.

43

While at home, William worked in his father's law office as an unpaid "gopher"—going to the Clerk's office for documents, to the county law library to run down bits of research, and to court simply to observe. One day at the Clerk's office he had to sign at the counter for some documents. Under the eye of the deputy clerk, his hand began to tremble. Soon, his whole body was shaking. But he finished his chore, and by time he was back in the office he was composed.

After dinner that evening, William and his father were sitting at opposite ends of the sun room sofa, each reading. His father laid down his newspaper and eased into conversation.

"I can remember when I worked summers while going to college back in Kansas. I was dispatcher for a building supply outfit on the edge of town. I'd get orders for supplies, see that the wagons were properly loaded, assign drivers for each load, and check the wagons back after each delivery. Although I was temporary, the drivers were long-time employees, a lot older than I and knew the layout a lot better. We got along well, and they helped me a lot. But there was one man who started riding me. Why, I don't know. But he'd make sarcastic remarks about me in front of the other men. Like things about my mother, and why didn't I get a job in a bank. That sort of thing. Everybody knew he was giving me a bad time, including my boss, and my boss finally asked me what was I going to do about it. So I cinched in my belt, and the next time he made a smart remark, I told him he was fired."

William had been looking directly at his father while his father spoke. He didn't have to be told that the deputy clerk before whom he had trembled that morning must have spoken to his father.

"Why are you telling me this?" William's voice dripped vitriol.

William and his father looked at each other without speaking.

William slammed his book down on the coffee table and walked from the room. His father picked up his newspaper and resumed reading.

14

William became bored with his role in his father's office, and when his brother-in-law mentioned an opening for a mathematician in the engineering division of the aircraft company where he worked, William jumped at the opportunity.

William had had a somewhat strange dual major in college—government and mathematics. He had taken all available courses in math for the pure love of the subject. Math was easy for him, he did well in it, and he enjoyed the mental stimulus. His job with the aircraft company suited him well.

Military needs had pressured the development of new and stronger alloys for fabricating aircraft. But when designers sought to take advantage of the new strength, they often confronted failure. A new alloy would not bend or stretch to the same limitations as would the old alloys that had been the subject of decades of use. The engineers wanted to develop some simple tests that would predict how an alloy would perform in fabrication. The tiny unit for which William was employed in the engineering division had been assigned the job of developing such tests. It was expected to be innovative.

The head of William's unit, Jim, was perfectly suited for his assigned task. He was not a trained engineer; he was not a careerist in the aircraft industry. He was a fiddler, an experimenter, an inventor of sorts. He and William struck it off well. William had developed over the years the defensive device of lightly challenging people who might be a threat and then ingratiating himself. Jim responded well to this approach.

As always, William was somewhat less than fully honest. When Jim noted that William never drank when the two of them stopped at a drinking fountain, William said that he was training for the time when he got thirsty and there was no water available. This was far from true; William didn't drink because the neurosurgeon had instructed him to severely limit his liquid intake.

Jim, an only child who still lived with his parents, invited William to dinner at his home. After the evening meal, Jim showed William his workshop. He had tools for woodworking and for both metal and electrical work. He had both a circular saw and a jig-saw. He had two lathes—one for wood and one for metal. He could solder, weld, heat-treat, punch, and rivet.

"You've got it all! If our company goes *kaput*, you're ready to fill the gap." Jim was pleased.

There was one part of William's job in which he was very uncomfortable. The testing lab was part of the production division—separate from the engineering division. William's unit frequently needed tests run and its staff, which consisted solely of Jim, William, and a young recently graduated engineer, would go to the lab with work orders for the tests. Two long-time employees of the company ran the lab. Jim got along well with them, and they liked working with him—possibly because was not an engineer, did not have any credentials to flaunt, and he both understood and appreciated the nature of their work. Whatever a work-order said, he would be able to work out with them, face-to-face, a practical program. William and the other young associate did not have this facility, and the two old hands loved giving them the run-around. They would send the two youngsters to get unneeded sign-offs on their orders or to get non-existent parts. All fun and games. Jim was furious when he learned of the high jinks, and gave the two lab men a dressing down. Even though the climate changed drastically, William never felt comfortable with the two men in the lab.

Jim left the company to enlist in the Navy not many months after William had arrived. They corresponded—William updating Jim on the work at the plant and Jim telling of his Navy experience. As he always had in correspondence, William assumed a light, joking style, bordering on the sarcastic, but never going over the line. The correspondence lagged—mainly on Jim's side. William learned from others that Jim was coming by the plant on a particular day to say goodby before shipping out.

When Jim came to the Engineering Division, he and his old friends met at picnic tables in front of the employee cafeteria. Jim had already been to the main plant. William and several others were seated at the tables when Jim arrived, and they stood to greet him. Jim shook hands with everyone but William. He didn't speak to William. He didn't look at him. When he sat down, William sat near him.

After friendly banter, Jim's former co-workers listened to his account of his navy experience—induction, boot-camp, drill, his buddies, barracks, mess detail, small arms, selection for a commission, and finally orders to ship out. There were questions and willing answers from Jim. But he afforded no word or glance to William. William could not stay silent.

"When you're not shooting at Japs, will they let you run experiments on the 16-inch guns?"

Jim turned toward William and narrowed his long red lashes over his sky-blue eyes.

"Still at it, eh?"

Something exploded in the back of William's mind. It would be years before he finished sweeping up the debris.

15

The same year, 1944, that Jim had met with his former co-workers at the plant, William received a long-distance call from his mother. His father had suffered a stroke and was being taken that day to the same hospital for examination by the same neurosurgeon who had examined William. Next day's examination disclosed that his father had a brain tumor. The neurosurgeon would operate the following day. His father could not walk and his only chance of walking again was removal of the tumor. He said he would be unable to practice law from a wheelchair and wanted the operation. William flew to San Francisco but arrived at the hospital after the operation. His mother took him to the hospital room where his father lay unconscious amid a tangle of tubes. His head was swathed in white bandage, and he was breathing heavily. The tumor had been determined malignant, and the neurosurgeon had been unable to remove it. He said that if his father survived he would be incapacitated. The surgeon also said that a major negative factor in his recovery was his father's overwhelming fear.

After showing William his father, William's mother sat with William to discuss the future. William had already decided to leave the aircraft company and seek a job at the University under a professor who was conducting research similar to what William had worked on at the aircraft company and who on a visit to the company had said to William that if he ever decided to leave the company to let him know. William now decided that he would leave the company to be nearer his mother, and he made an appointment to meet with the professor the next day.

In returning from his appointment with the professor, William walked up a long sidewalk toward the hospital entrance. He saw his mother come out of the Hospital with his sister and a long-time family friend, herself a widowed mother, in whose home his mother was staying. His mother was leaning on his sister. William realized at once that his father had died. He hurried ahead and put his arms around his mother. Neither spoke, but his sister did.

"You could have been here instead of running around on errands!" William did not respond, but their family friend spoke for him.

"You were doing just what your father would have wanted you to do."

Back in the friend's home, William, his mother and his sister talked a bit about the immediate future. The funeral would be in their hometown. William's sister would make the necessary arrangements, would arrange publication of a death notice, and would contact friends and relatives who should be notified. William would return to his job.

William's mother said that if William decided to attend law school, she would finance him "even if she had to scrub toilets." He told her that would be unnecessary, and vowed to himself that he would accept no money from her at all.

* * *

William decided that he would leave his job with the aircraft company and enroll in law school. He figured that his accumulated savings, plus summer employment, plus part-time work on campus would be sufficient to carry him through three years in a state school that charged no tuition. The only cost would be for food, lodging, books, and student fees. And he would be engaged in what he had always excelled—academic study.

He proved right about the finances. He was able to rent a bare room for $25 per month, eat a 34 cent breakfast consisting of two bowls of oatmeal, fix his own lunch, and eat a hot dinner at a student co-op for about $30 per month. He bought assigned textbooks in used condition, and did not indulge in the purchase of any study aids. He had no social life.

But he was wrong about the academics. He had great trouble concentrating, and no matter how much time he spent preparing written briefs of all assigned cases and distilling the results into written outlines, he felt he had a poor grasp of his subjects. His mid-year grades were a disaster. He got a D in one subject and C in all others. In short, he had gone down grade points and would flunk out if he kept on this course. Fear of failure rode like a screaming monkey on his back.

One night, he dreamt that his supervisor at the aircraft plant, Jim, came through his door. William had balanced a full bucket of water on the top of the partly opened door, and when Jim opened it further the bucket tumbled, drenching him from head to foot.

William also hallucinated during the day. When walking toward a fire hydrant he often hallucinated that he would step over the hydrant, scraping his testicles off on the top of the hydrant.

One day in December he was standing on the sidewalk at the corner Telegraph Avenue and Durant Street trying to decide which way to turn in shopping for Christmas gifts for his family and friends. As he stood, he envisioned in his hands the 20 gauge shotgun that had exploded in his hands years before. He was raising the gun to his head, his left thumb on the trigger. When the muzzle reached his forehead, he began pressing the trigger. Suddenly, the vision vanished like a bursting bubble. Bathed in cold sweat, William turned on his heel to finish his shopping in a blanket of fear.

* * *

As he finished his first year, William decided he would write an article for publication in the school's law review. The best student scholars were "elected" to the law review and if elected were expected to contribute at least one scholarly article for publication in the review, which was widely circulated among and read by practicing lawyers throughout the state. Each student writer had a faculty "advisor" for each article. William made an appointment with his favorite professor to recruit him as an advisor and to select a topic for an article. The professor, who was perhaps the nation's foremost legal scholar in his area of specialty, readily gave William an appointment, but when they were together gently pushed him to take some R&R time in the summer rather than doing more legal research and study. It was obvious to William that the professor thought him too over-wrought and anxious from his last school year and that he should back off. William demurred, saying he simply did not have time for this sort of thing during the school year, and he wanted to do it. So they selected a topic, and the professor pointed him in the right direction.

* * *

Townsend felt he had about reached his limit. He raised with his mother the possibility that he skip the next year of law school and spend the year back-packing the length of the California coast.

"And then what do you do?"

"I don't know what I'd do. Maybe when I'm through, I'd have it sorted out."

"That sounds like a bad idea. I think you shouldn't let go of what you're doing without knowing what's next. Some of our friends think you have become so withdrawn you should get some professional counseling."

"No, I'm not going to do that." But William finished his law review article that summer and returned to law school. His faculty advisor liked his article, and it was published.

* * *

First semester of his second year William signed up to audit a tennis gym class. He hoped that disciplined exercise might help clear his head. It may have helped a little, but not much. Second semester he signed up for basketball. He also decided to make an appointment with the chief of neurosurgery who had examined him after his epileptic seizure while in college and who had operated on his father.

The chief of neurosurgery somehow reminded Townsend of Earl Warren. He was a big, bear of a man with smooth features exuding both strength and geniality.

"It's good to see you. How's your mother?"

"All considered, she's doing well. She's taken a couple of trips and is planning more. She sees some of your family once in awhile at gatherings."

"How has it been going in law school?" William was tight as a drum.

"Not well. My grades have been very poor."

"Anything wrong?"

"Not really."

William and the physician stared at each other.

"Oh? I'm sorry to hear that. What's the trouble?"

"I can't focus very well and I don't retain what I study."

"Are you still taking the phenobarbital?"

"Yes. I meant to ask about it. Can I stop?"

"Yes, you can stop. Also see about restoring your driver's license. If you need a letter from me, I'll give you one."

"Also, I want to ask you about exercise. I've signed up for a basketball class, and we're going at it pretty hard."

"That's fine. Engage in even violent exercise. If you have a problem, give me a call."

William and the physician looked at each other again in silence.

"Have you had any sexual intercourse?"

"No, sir."

"Have you attempted any?"

"No, sir."

"O.K., is there anything else you would like to raise with me?"

"No, sir. Thank you for seeing me."

William had a feeling of relief as he descended the hospital steps. Boarding a bus headed for the Ferry Building, he took a window seat. At the next stop, a young girl with a white cane boarded the bus and, after some exploratory poking with the tip of her cane, carefully lowered herself into the seat next to William.

"You're pretty handy with that cane. Have you been blind all your life?"

"Yes, I was born blind."

"Why don't you get a guide dog?"

"I'm going to, but I want to learn to get around San Francisco on my own first. Here's where I get off."

Laying a hand on William's arm, the girl gave him a warm smile, rose, and got off the bus.

* * *

Despite his errant thoughts, William forced himself to focus sufficiently on his studies that his school performance gradually improved. The D that William had received in Criminal Law his first semester was the last D he received in law school. By graduation his average had reached somewhere between B and C. Not good, but not a disaster.

16

William had headed home to stay with his mother for the summer. She had had a room with a private bath added to her new home specifically to accommodate William. He knew she hoped he would eventually return to their hometown to practice law and that he would live with her.

William arranged to work the summer at the minimum wage on the fruit farm of his mother's uncle, located about thirty miles away. He had the use of a Model-A pickup truck to drive back and forth. There were some resident workers on the farm, migrants from Oklahoma during the depression years, but most of the fruit pickers during the summer were seasonal workers from Mexico who lived in a large dormitory and prepared their own meals. William wondered if they were legally in the country and if they were being paid the minimum wage.

William had two principal jobs on the farm. When apples or pears were being picked, he drove a team of two horses with a flat-bed wagon up and down the rows picking up full boxes of fruit and dropping off empties. One day William stopped on a slight uphill slope with a full load of empties. He tied the reins to a stanchion on the front of the wagon, jumped down, and went to the rear of the wagon. He stepped up on the wagon floor and loosened the ropes tying the load. As he did so, the end tier of boxes tipped back, sending William to the ground in a jumble of empty boxes. The pickers observed all of this from their ladders with obvious amusement. William emerged from the boxes, brushed himself off, said nothing, and proceeded to stack the boxes at their intended delivery point. He didn't look at the pickers. From that time on, William and the pickers exchanged huge grins whenever they spoke to each other.

"Quiere cajones?"

"Si, si!"

"Que quante?"

"Ocho."

William's mastery of Spanish from a single semester of study back in junior high school may not have been perfect, but he was communicating.

William's other job was during berry season. The children from the families living on the farm were sent to the berry fields to supplement their family's income through piece-rate pay for picking. William was assigned to supervise the children. Each morning he drove his model-A pickup with a load of empty crates to the berry-field of the day. He would also carry in the back of the truck as many of the twenty-or-so children as he could. The rest would walk. He would assign the children their rows, see that they picked their rows clean without picking unripe berries, gently empty the berries from their picking buckets into crates, and record the amount picked by each child. The children were directed not to throw clods or engage in any other horse-play. They were in the fields to work.

Almost all the children in William's crew were both docile and diligent. However, there was one boy, Billie, who was a rebel. He would rush through his row, leaving it but partly picked, and was constantly shouting at other pickers. Despite admonishment by William, he threw clods. He was a holy terror.

After his father's death, William's mother had purchased a vacation cabin on the ocean some fifty miles from her home. While William was home during law school vacation, he and his mother often drove to the cabin on a weekend to perform necessary maintenance and simply to enjoy the ocean. During one such drive, while William was at the wheel of her car, he told his mother of his problems with Billie. His mother had been a school teacher and reputedly a very good disciplinarian. After some discussion, William's mother told him that he would simply have to cinch in his belt and "take control."

"You've never told me *that*, Mother." His voice dripped sarcasm. Neither of them spoke the rest of the ride.

That evening at the cabin, William and his mother played a game of scrabble in front of the fireplace. William excused himself relatively early and went upstairs to the loft to turn in. The loft was open to the downstairs and William could see down to the fireplace. He looked downstairs before getting in bed and saw his mother playing a game of solitaire where the two of them had been sitting. Tears were streaming down her face.

William went to sleep. He dreamt that he was downstairs, an axe clutched in his two hands. He was hacking at his mother.

Next week at the ranch, William had another confrontation with Billie. A temporary privy was located next to the berry patch. When William saw that Billie was missing from his row, he went to the privy and through a crack saw Billy sitting on the john reading a comic book. William looked around for a slat from a berry crate. When he found one, he picked it up and returned to the privy.

"Come out here!"

Startled, Billie put down his comic book and came out.

"Bend over and grab your knees."

Billie bent over, all the time protesting.

"You can't whip me; I'll tell my folks!"

"Grab your knees."

At this point, William's principal fear was that he would flub his stroke with the slat. He needn't have worried. He laid on a beauty. Billie would not only have felt the sting through his blue jeans, but no doubt had a healthy welt on his bottom.

William tossed the slat aside and strode away without another word.

"I'm going to tell my folks!"

William walked to the pickup and drove away, leaving the children unattended. He drove to the apple-grader near the main ranch house where he knew Billie's mother was working. William's grand-uncle happened to be working with her, tossing out bad apples.

"I just gave your son Billie a whipping."

"What did he do?"

"He's been regularly raising cane in the berry patch. This time he went to the privy to spend his time reading a comic book when he should have been in the patch. I decided I had had enough."

"Thank you for telling me."

William got in his pickup and drove back to the berry patch. All of the children, including Billie, were dutifully picking their rows and did not look up. The work-day finished without a murmur. When the children piled on the truck, Billie got into the front seat next to William. Neither of them spoke on the ride back. William had no doubt Billie would get another licking at home. At any rate, from that time on Billie was the very model of a perfect berry picker—diligent, obedient, and a willing helper to his field boss.

* * *

William cemented his relations with the ranch foreman early on. Pat had fled his Oklahoma farm with his family during the dust-bowl years and had long served as the much-respected and much-liked foreman. One day in the midst of apple-picking, a clap of thunder and a darkening sky announced a coming storm. The pickers hurried to get the boxes of picked apples on William's flat-bed and under cover. Pat drove up in his pickup and motioned William to get in. William got in, curious to see where they were going. The pickers kept loading the flat-bed. Pat drove to the main ranch house. Neither spoke.

"Get out and go in."

"What for?"

"It's starting to rain."

"The other men aren't stopping."

"They're used to it."

"How did they get used to it?"

"…You don't want to go in?"

"No."

Pat slapped William on the knee, put the pickup in gear, made a u-turn, and drove back to the orchard.

As clear as crystal, William could see his Aunt Mary's hand in the farm management.

17

While living with his mother during the summers between his law school years, William planted and maintained a vegetable garden in a vacant lot between his mother's home and their next neighbor. The daughter of the couple next door had a nervous disorder that rendered her spastic. On her own premises she could get about with a walker, but otherwise used an electric wheel chair. Apart from her disorder she was a handsome girl, with long black hair in a bun, peaches and cream complection, a generous figure, large eyes that were widely spaced, and a ready smile. Both her head and her limbs moved convulsively. Her speech was seriously impaired but understandable.

The kitchen windows of both William's and Beverly's homes opened onto the Townsend vegetable garden. When William first turned the soil and planted the garden, Beverly came out of her back kitchen door.

"Wh-what are you d-doing?"

"Planting a garden. Any objection?"

"N-no, no. It's O.k.k. with me. I d-don't own this land."

"Maybe you can help me with the garden. It will need more watering than I can give it."

Thus commenced William's and Beverly's gardening relationship. Whenever William came out of his house to weed, water, or harvest, odds were that Beverly would appear at her kitchen door.

"How are the zu-zu-zuchini doing?"

"Doing fine. But giving me a bad time. Every time those buggers see me come out of the house, they duck under the leaves. Don't like being picked. Look at the size of this one! Should have been picked a week ago. Here, you can have it."

"D-d-don't want it. You always t-t-try to g-g-give me the big t-t-tough ones."

"Well, pick what you want. Just don't let them get away. Same with the beans and the lettuce. Doesn't matter with tomatoes. No way they can hide when they're ripe. I think, though, the mailman may be swiping some. Keep an eye open. If he's why we don't get many tomatoes, I'll report him."

"Oh, M-m-mister Townsend, you would-d-dn't report the m-m-mailman! I t-t-told him he c-c-could take all the t-t-tomatoes he wanted."

"You can't do that without my agreement! You're doing hardly any of the work."

And so it went. Beverly loved to tease and be teased. William suspected she got very little of it.

* * *

Standing at her kitchen sink, William's mother often saw William and Beverly in the vegetable garden. One day at lunch his mother broached the subject.

"You and Beverly seem to have struck up quite a friendship."

"Yes, we have. We enjoy each other. I don't think she has a chance to develop many friends."

"You'll want to keep it a bit arms length. Teenage girls with her type of disorder have a reputation for sexual precocity. If she gets pregnant, you might get blamed."

Townsend and his mother looked at each other in stony silence. When he had cleaned his plate, he took it to the sink, ran some water over it, and walked from the room.

William made a point thereafter of being sure that Beverly knew when he was in the vegetable garden.

18

William's brief exchange with his mother concerning Beverly and sexuality was not his first exchange with his mother about sex and would not be the last.

While reading a biography of Tchaikovsky during his junior high, William ran onto the word "homosexual." He asked his mother what it meant. She said she didn't know. She did not refer him to a dictionary.

When William was a freshman it high school, his mother sat him down in the sun room for what was obviously going to be a very serious conversation.

"Your father has said he was going to talk to you about girls and dating, but he keeps putting it off, and I don't think he's ever going to do it. So I have decided I should do it.

"The human body is a wonderful and beautiful thing. Small wonder the Greek sculptors depicted it in their works of art. It is nothing to be ashamed of. It should be appreciated. You will be attracted to girls because of the beauty of their bodies, but that doesn't mean that you love them. You have got to understand the difference between attraction and loving. Eventually, you will love and hopefully marry some woman, and you should save yourself for that. Your dad says that you can tell the difference between loving and simply wanting a woman by whether you want to protect her. In any event, he says he has been helped in keeping his life straight by reading a book that I am giving you."

His mother handed him a slim volume titled *As a Man Thinketh*. William took it.

"Do you have any questions?"

"No." William left the room.

* * *

While still working at the aircraft company and before attending law school, William had another exchange with his mother concerning sexual matters. He had in a pocket of his blue jeans a condom that had been surreptitiously inserted by one of the lodgers in the boarding house in which he lived in Santa Monica. When he came on it, he left it in his pocket. In time, he became concerned that his mother, who did his laundry when he was home, might have come on it. His concern soon hardened into a conviction that she had. While driving her on a jaunt to San Francisco, he raised the subject.

"You may have seen a condom in the pocket of my blue jeans."

"A *what*?"

"A condom. A rubber contraceptive."

"Why in the world would I see any such thing?"

"Because there's one there. I think I should explain."

"Go ahead and explain, but I have no idea what you're talking about."

By now it was clear to William that his mother had not seen it, and would probably have had no idea what it was if she had.

"I didn't put it there and have no idea who did, but it must have been a joke by one of my house mates down in Santa Monica."

"Why is it a joke?"

"Because they think it's probably the last thing in the world I would be carrying around."

"So?"

There seemed no way to get out of this conversation.

"I just thought I should tell you."

19

While in high school, William had fallen into the habit of not exerting any personal rights or privileges. His model was the protagonist in Tolstoy's *War and Peace*, who was maneuvered into accepting a challenge to a duel and then fired his dueling pistol into the ground and simply awaited his opponent's shot. If William was wronged, that was the wrong-doer's problem, not his. Once, when William had sold some of his postage stamps to another collector but had not been paid, his parents told him that he should insist on payment. He refused to make any demand. He simply would not engage in any form of confrontation. But in starting a legal career, William knew he was headed toward a profession in which confrontation was the name of the game. More deeply, he realized that his avoidance of confrontation was a weakness, not a virtue.

After the death of William's father, his mother had applied for survivor's benefits under Social Security but her application was denied. This seemed superficially reasonable because, after all, the law had been designed to provide a financial safety net for those of little income and assets, not for the relatively affluent such as William's family. On reading the statute, William became convinced that his mother had been wrongly denied benefits. His father had engaged in "self-employment" in purchasing a local prune orchard and developing it as a real estate project. He had declared and paid "self-employment" tax for social security on his earnings. His surviving spouse was clearly entitled to benefits. Or so William thought. He decided to act on his mother's behalf. But doing so required that he go to the local SSA office and confront its staff. He did so and succeeded in obtaining his mother's benefits.

Another outgrowth of the prune orchard venture brought William to another confrontation. Wartime demand for dried prunes had generated an abnormal demand for drying trays and the supply of trays was short. Hence the inflated value of a hundred or so unused trays stacked in the former prune orchard. Acting for his mother, William placed a "for sale" ad in the local paper. A prune grower located about ten miles from town responded, met with William to inspect the trays, agreed on the price, and promised William he would pick up the trays the following day and give William the check for his mother. He failed to show up as promised. William knew from his recent law school course in contracts that his mother had a legally enforceable contract with the grower. He got in his mother's car, drove to the home of the grower, and rang the door-bell. With the long-familiar sinking feeling in the pit of his stomach, William explained to the grower that he had already bought the trays and William asked him for a check. The grower wrote the check and said he would pick up his trays next day. William's head sang with relief.

A third confrontational event is worth noting. Near the end of William's third year in law school, his class scheduled the traditional class picnic. Although William had had essentially no personal contact with his classmates during three years in law school and knew he was regarded by them as some sort of oddball, he was resolved to participate in their group activities. He accordingly packed himself a lunch and got himself by public transportation and walking to the picnic site. Once there, he joined in the baseball game, although he had never played baseball and had only a dim understanding of the rules. When his turn came at the plate he surprisingly made contact with the ball and threw down his bat as he raced to first base. His bat hit the opposing catcher on the foot. William returned to home plate and apologized to the catcher, a husky, somewhat florid young man and former navy officer named Muldoon. When William again came up, he again made contact, threw down his bat for the race to first, and again hit the catcher on his foot. This time, the catcher erupted.

"You son of a bitch! Are you trying to kill me?"

William, who had been easily beaten out by the throw to first, walked back to home plate and stood silently in front of the still ranting catcher. When the catcher wound down, William picked up his bat and walked away.

Muldoon and William were both in opening class the following Monday. When Muldoon took his seat, which was some distance from William's, William walked over, stood directly in front of him, and said that he was sorry he had hit his foot with the bat. Muldoon said he understood and he was sorry for what he had said to William.

William also went to the senior class ball before graduation. Although this required scrounging up a date, it required less effort than he had feared. In any event, however ill he had fitted into his class, he remained resolved not to avoid any of its activities.

William's mother and a surviving partner of his father's law firm attended his commencement. The ceremony was held in the university football stadium, with the graduates seated in groups on the playing field. The commencement speaker was the then Secretary of State Robert McNamara, and security was tight. Graduates from each of the constituent colleges were graduated in groups *en masse*. Although William could not see his mother in the stands, he knew she was proud.

20

Next on William's agenda was preparing for the state bar examination. He moved home with a three years' accumulation of class notes and his personal course summaries. He would spend the summer studying and practicing for the three day bar examination that would be held in San Francisco in October.

William divided each day between review of his law school materials at home and study in the law library at the county courthouse. He allocated three days to each semester's subject at law school. He reserved a half-day of mini-review on each subject at the end. Finally, he ear-marked time to for a self-administered, timed practice exam on each subject that would be covered, or might be covered, in the actual bar exam. At the end of this scheduled study and practice he reserved a full week of R&R to permit his arrival in San Francisco in October rested and ready to go.

William held to his schedule, but was broke by October. Despite having vowed not to do so, he touched his mother for a loan to cover bus fare and a three night stay in the City. She was more than willing to oblige. William had a sneaky feeling that there had been a streak of meanness in his earlier refusal to accept anything from her, and that she felt somewhat relieved at his having finally asked for some cash. He did, however, fully repay the loan, and a few other small loans, when he was finally employed.

Despite his anxiety, which no doubt was shared with all others taking the exam, William was confident he had done everything possible to succeed. His confidence was not misplaced, and when he came out of the exam he was equally confident he had passed.

* * *

Now, how to start work as an attorney? William knew that his law school record made him an unattractive candidate for a position with a major law firm. Although the two remaining partners in his father's old firm had invited him to join them, he was resolved not to return to his hometown to follow his father's footsteps and live with his mother. He would locate somewhere else. He researched the national directory of lawyers and law firms to identify every firm in San Francisco with an "a-v" rating, the highest. With a list of names, addresses and telephone numbers of the top fifty to a hundred firms, he intended to pound the pavement and knock on doors. So, again borrowing from his mother for bus fare, he saw, or attempted to see, every hiring partner on his list of firms. Completely depressing. Only one expressed even sympathetic interest. He would contact William—but never did.

Back home after five days pounding the streets of San Francisco, William recounted his experience to a partner in his dad's old firm.

"Just what you should have expected. I can get a job for you with a D.A. I've worked with and is a good friend. Do you want me to?"

Chagrined, William said he would appreciate it. The partner reached for the phone.

"Hello, Frank. This is Owen. I have young William Townsend sitting in front of me. He just took the bar exam and has been looking for a job in the City. Pretty discouraging. I would like you to give him a job in your office until he can get his feet on the ground. Yes, I know you're constricted on funds, but you can create a job if you try. O.K., he'll call for an appointment."

William had just had a lesson in how to get along in the real world.

"Frank will give you a job, but it probably won't pay much. Do you want my secretary to call for an appointment?"

When William walked into the office of the District Attorney, Frank was sitting behind a huge mahogany desk. He got up, walked around his desk, shook hands, and gestured William to a chair. Resuming his own seat, he reminisced a bit about his working days with Owen, reminisced a bit about William's father, and then turned to the subject of William's visit.

"Owen tells me you've been pounding the pavement in San

Francisco. It's pretty tough right now. Graduating law classes are small, but there are a lot of lawyers returning from service. He wants me to give you a job as a deputy D.A. in this office. I can do that, but I can't pay you much. The most we can pay you is $100 before deductions. That leaves you with about $75."

William felt that the D.A. would as soon he turn down the offer, but with his S.F. experience he was not about to turn anything down.

"I would like to work with you. I'm not concerned about the size of the pay. When I was in law school I had an evening job at the Women's City Club on their dishwasher in exchange for three meals a day. I'm sure I can get the same job again, and your pay will permit me to get by."

The D.A. shuffled the papers on his desk.

"I'm not going to have any deputy of mine working on a dishwasher."

William thought to himself, *Fat chance. If you won't pay me enough to live on, your not going to tell me what work I can do off the job.*

William both took the job at the D.A.'s office and reapplied for his old evening job on the dishwasher. Unhappily, he couldn't get the job with the Women's City Club because he couldn't get away from his lawyering job in time to meet their dishwashing schedule. Instead, he got a job teaching mathematics and physics in adult evening school. He assumed even the D.A. would approve.

William moved back to the Bay Area, rented another $25 room with a single light bulb hanging from the ceiling, and began his career as a lawyer.

21

William was assigned to a branch of the District Attorney's office located in the Oakland City Hall. The City Hall office handled misdemeanors, both the filing of charges and trials, and preliminary hearings in felonies. The City Hall was an old building and the D.A.'s quarters were both crowded and grungy. Both the commercial and governmental center of the city had shifted since the City Hall had been built and it was now in a neighborhood consisting largely of cleaners, laundries, bondsmen, drug stores, mercantile banks, insurance offices, real estate offices, lunch counters, restaurants, and a couple of large old theaters—all located in pre-war buildings. The City Hall itself was of solid granite, finished inside in hardwood, with marble floors in the public areas. It was overcrowded, with no central air-conditioning and many areas originally intended to be open were now partitioned into small cubicles, each with a desk and a couple of chairs. The interior smelled vaguely of oily sawdust, furniture polish, and dust. A buzz of constant activity bounced back from a painted tin ceiling.

The City Hall housed the Mayor's office, his immediate staff, the Municipal Courts, the Municipal Probation Office, the lockup, the Central Division of the Oakland Police Department, and various smaller offices of the city government that couldn't be squeezed in anywhere else. The City Hall Office of the District Attorney's Office, which served as municipal prosecutor, was on the second floor for ready access to the public and the courts.

When Townsend reported for his first day of work, he was greeted at the counter by a dark haired, somewhat stout young lady, who introduced herself with a big smile as "Julie."

"Please have a seat. The Prosecutor would like to see you as soon as he finishes talking with Captain Bolger. They should be through any minute. Would you like a cup of fresh coffee?"

A uniformed captain of police emerged from the prosecutor's office within the next five minutes. Julie took him firmly in hand.

"Captain, this is William Townsend, a new recruit in our office."

"Hi, William. I'm glad to meet you. We can use all the lawyers we can get. When you can, I hope you will drop by my office so we can get acquainted and I can tell you something about the police department."

Just then, the prosecutor came out of his office door.

"Hello, Mr. Townsend. I'm sorry to keep you waiting. Come in."

The office was small, unlike that of the District Attorney in the County Court House. It had a linoleum floor, a medium size desk with a swivel chair, an armchair, a table with three straight chairs, a large glass-front book case bulging with black binders and printed codes, two file cabinets, a coatrack and a window air-conditioner.

The prosecutor looked to be about forty years, smooth shaved, graying hair, with a sprightly, friendly air.

"We have a desk for you, but not a private office. As you will see, we are pretty cramped. We may have an office for you later, but don't count on it. Our law library is housed in Judge Kennedy's chambers, and I will show it to you today. You are assigned to Traffic Court, and George Reid, who is presently assigned, will go to Court tomorrow morning to introduce you to Judge Smith. George will give you your case files for tomorrow and will take you around to the clerk and introduce you to the bailiff. He will also fill you in on what you need to know about court procedures. Julie will lead you through the personnel maze and will introduce you to the rest of our staff. Any questions?"

"I expect I'll have a lot, but I'll dump them on George and Julie."

"O.K., let's go."

Thus began Townsend's career as a lawyer among careerists who took their jobs very seriously, but did not, by and large, take themselves very seriously. He didn't know it at the time, but he could not have started better.

After a short stint in non-jury traffic court, William was assigned his first jury trial—a prosecution for driving while under the influence of alcohol, or "DUI." State law at that time mandated suspension of a defendant's drivers license upon conviction of DUI, and for that reason there were few guilty pleas and many defendants with competent trial lawyers. Also, proof was difficult because the police were not yet administering blood or breath tests for the presence of alcohol. Rather, they subjected an arrested driver to a standard set of "sobriety" tests— walking a straight line, touching one's nose with arms outstretched and eyes closed, letting the arresting officer smell his breath, and answering questions about where he had been and how many and what drinks he had had. And even then, an arrestee could choose not to cooperate. Whether he did or didn't, a skilled defense attorney would almost surely get an acquittal.

William was not expected to get a conviction, and he didn't. In reviewing the case file the evening before trial, he was reminded that the defendant was a handsome young man, recently married, and with no prior record of arrest. The defendant and his wife had a six month old baby girl, and the mother and child would surely appear in the front row of the spectator section throughout the trial. Perhaps the most critical emotional factor favoring acquittal was the defendant's employment as a milk wagon driver. License suspension meant job loss. He had been arrested at 7:35 p.m., when visibility was minimal, shortly after leaving an informal birthday celebration for a co-worker. It had been raining. The bartender said (and his friends at the tavern could be expected to say) that he was sober when he left. The officers had pulled him over when they saw his car weaving. He could be expected to testify that he was very tired and became distracted. He told the officers he had had only two beers.

William's mind was in turmoil when went to sleep the evening before trial. He dreamt that the defendant was on the witness stand, his wife and baby beside him. The defendant was in the immaculate white uniform of a milk wagon driver. His wife wore a modest, very prim dress, and the baby was whimpering. The defendant had the rapt attention of the jurors as he strummed a guitar and softly sang. William strained to hear. He was singing, "Paddling home by the light of the moon." That was his defense! He wasn't driving while intoxicated. He was simply paddling home by the light of the moon. Terror! William knew that his cross-examination of the defendant would be limited to the scope of the defendant's direct testimony. But William didn't even own a guitar—let alone know how to play one! He awoke in a cold sweat.

William's nightmare notwithstanding, the trial went well. The arresting officers made a good appearance and testified convincingly. At least William thought that the jurors should be convinced. And they were, but acquitted nonetheless. As the jurors filed out of the courtroom, a middle-aged woman juror patted the defendant on the shoulder, saying, "Son, don't do that again."

In that moment, William thought he knew that the jury system wouldn't and couldn't work. It was only later in his career he realized that this was the glory of the system and that it had worked very well in his DUI case.

* * *

After a couple of years in the City Hall office, William was brought back to the main office to join the felony trial staff. He tried all types of cases, including first-degree murder cases in which the death penalty was demanded. He had no qualms about the death penalty, but it was never ordered in any case that he tried. Accordingly, he was never compelled to face the question—as had other attorneys on the trial staff—of whether he should go to the state penitentiary to witness an execution he had requested. But over a period of three years, he had an unremitting string of convictions that gained him a reputation as a trial attorney. It was only after he had decided to leave the D.A.'s office that he suffered a couple of acquittals. The second of them—the last case that he tried as a deputy D.A.—is worth noting.

William's last case was a prosecution for mayhem. The defendant, a former professional wrestler, had been arrested for engaging in a barroom brawl and had resisted arrest. The arresting officers had used force in subduing him and in the resulting melee he bit off the lower portion of one officer's ear. The officers, understandably, pushed for prosecution to the limit, and the staff in the City Hall office obliged by charging the defendant not only with resisting arrest but with mayhem, a felony.

William knew from the case file that the defendant bore many contusions and abrasions from his struggle with the officers. He also knew that the defendant, on questioning, had claimed that he had been beaten by the officers with billy clubs. When William interviewed the officers in preparation for trial, they at first denied clubbing the defendant but then, under close questioning, admitted having used their clubs. William explained to them that it made no difference in terms of the defendant's guilt whether or not they used their clubs and that it was essential that they tell the full truth when they testified under oath in court. Each of them promised to testify to having used his club.

Under the pressure of court appearance, each of the officers reverted to form. Each solemnly denied using his club in any way, or even taking his club in hand. William held his tongue, and in closing argument told the jury that in judging the defendant's guilt of having deliberately disfigured the officer by biting off a portion of his ear it didn't matter whether the officers had or had not used their clubs. The public defender argued that the officers had lied about not using their clubs, and that their entire testimony was therefore suspect. In final argument William while forcefully making a point that "the defense would have you believe that these officers are liars…," said instead, "the defense would have you believe that these *liars* are…er, I mean these officers…." William's Freudian slip was not lost on the jurors. They took just thirty minutes to acquit. Back in his office, William gave the officers a stern lecture. What he should have done was send a written report to the chief of police leaving open the possibility of perjury prosecutions.

22

When joining the DA's office Townsend had assumed he would take vacations like everyone else. He should not have assumed. When Earl Warren, later Chief Justice, was district attorney for Alameda County during the depression years, his deputies received no salary. Rather, they were permitted to collect fees for a modicum of private practice they were allowed to conduct out of their public office space. No rent; no pay. Although such an arrangement would have seemed outlandish at the time Townsend went to work in the office, it was nonetheless thrown up to him as justifying no vacation his first summer.

"You expect to get a vacation when you haven't been working here even a year?"

"But I'm hardly paid."

"I know, but let me tell you something. Have you ever heard of Earl Warren?"

"Of course. He was DA of Alameda County. Then State AG. Now Governor. What's he got to do with me?"

"When he was DA, he didn't pay his deputies *anything*, but he didn't allow them *any* vacation until they had worked for two years."

"But I'm not working for Earl Warren, and it's not the depression. Please check with Frank."

At which Julie broke out laughing and scheduled William's vacation.

* * *

Townsend's first vacation while in the D.A.'s office was spent motoring up the northern California coast with his mother to enjoy scenery on a route neither had seen. One of their stops was at the mouth of the Klammath River during the fall run of salmon. Parking their car, they walked out on the sand spit separating the river from the ocean. There were many fishermen casting artificial lures, mostly silver spoons, down-current in the river and reeling back against the current with the hope the lure would be taken by a fish entering the river to spawn upstream. A few fishermen were fishing in the surf, and one venturesome pair was even in a rowboat with an outboard trolling just outside the surf. These two trollers would surface a part of William's past.

As with many toddlers, William had had the experience of stumbling in the shallow surf of a bathing beach, being rolled by the next wave, picked up by a watchful parent, and carried from the surf terrified and sobbing. Although he overcame, with parental help, the fear of the surf itself, it was years before he overcame fear of a lung full of water. Throughout high school he swam only by dog-paddling.

In his sophomore year at college, Townsend's dorm room window overlooked the college swimming pool. In warm weather he could both see and hear the swimming instruction. He decided to visit the pool during quiet hours and start teaching himself to swim. It was easier than he had anticipated. With his feet firmly on the bottom, he learned to turn his head to the left, inhale air through his open mouth, then turn his head down and expel breath through his nose underwater. Floating face down, he did the same on the surface. It was a short step, indeed a necessary step, to stroking with his arms in rhythm with his breathing. And then kicking from his thighs. Put it all together, and he was swimming the Australian crawl! In short order, he was also swimming the breast stroke and the side stroke. He built up his strength and endurance in all three styles. He turned to diving, but hit a brick wall. Although he could force himself to roughly execute a back dive, a forward flip, a half-gainer, and one or two other rudimentary dives, he always came out of them with a one-quarter to one-half twist. It dawned on him this was because of asymmetry of his body due to his childhood meningitis. No amount of practice would cure or correct it.

When he had worked at Douglas Aircraft in Santa Monica during the war William had lived only two blocks from the beach. In his first summer he began swimming in the surf on arriving home from work. It was a friendly activity, and there were still a few swimmers on the beach or in the water when he arrived. He felt none of his childhood stress. His initial alarm at seeing shark-like dorsal fins cruising toward him was quickly replaced by the comforting realization they belonged to curiously friendly porpoises simply wanting to swim with him.

In the fall, with the end of daylight savings, he found himself swimming each day in the dusk and eventually in the dark. He learned that when the water turned to a milky brown in the fall, it was not from mud, but from swarms of phosphorescent algae that glowed in the dark when disturbed. Beyond the breakers, if William swept an arm through the inky water at night it would leave a golden arc of phosphorescence.

On most weekends in Santa Monica, William swam in daylight. He would swim the approximate quarter-mile out to the breakwater, haul himself out on the rocks to warm in the sun and rest for his swim back. His childhood fear of the water was gone. Its total disappearance would be confirmed on his vacation trip with his mother up the California coast when working in the Alameda County D.A.'s office.

While William and his mother watched the fishermen on the river side of the sand spit at the mouth of the Klamath, they noticed some of them rush over to the ocean side. The two men in the rowboat, now just beyond the surf, were waving their oars. Their outboard motor was not working. One of the men took up the oars and was turning the boat so it's prow would face the incoming breakers that were propelling it to the beach. He succeeded in getting the boat turned just in time to top a breaker. In the meantime, people on the beach were forming a human chain—each man grasping the wrist of the next to advance, man-by-man, out to the two men in the boat. William hurriedly took off his shoes and ran out to take a place at the head of the chain. He firmly took hold of the wrist of the leader and the man grasped William's wrist. Although the second man in the rowboat had moved to the stern, which should have provided more stability, the next breaker lifted the boat and threw it forward up-side-down. The man in the stern managed to gain his footing in the surf and came thrashing ashore. The rower lay upside down in the slack water between waves. William immediately jerked his hand free and ran in slack water to the rower. As he started to lift the man from the armpit, the number two man from the human chain started lifting from the other side. Between the two of them, they managed to hold on to the unconscious man, maintain their footing, and drag the man to the beach.

Those on the beach had already laid out a blanket on which the co-rescuers laid the unconscious man for artificial respiration. He quickly revived. William walked over to dry himself near a blazing beach fire. Another person standing near the fire pointed at the sopping William and asked whether he was the "hero" or the "fool." Assured that William was the "hero," the questioner gave William a broad smile. William couldn't understand why he was bereft of fear in splashing out to the drowning man. He didn't feel at all like a "hero." What he had done seemed to have come naturally. But it left him feeling comfortable with himself.

23

William's next two vacations were solo camping trips in the Sierra Nevada. Although he was enjoying the hustle and bustle of work around the courts, he also enjoyed getting off by himself for a spell in the woods fishing the streams. The first of these trips was to Yosemite. He drove to the Awani on the south rim of the valley, locked his car, shouldered his pack and took off. He had current trail maps from U.S. Geodetic Survey and knew exactly the route he would take over Vogelsang Pass and then back to the Merced River.

Camping was a very different exercise than it had been when he was in high school more than twenty years before. No more army blanket, no more fir boughs for bedding, no more canned goods or raw potatoes and onions. He carried a one man shelter tent, a down mummy bag, a torso-length inflatable mattress, a single-burner Coleman stove, and freeze-dried food. Camping in comfort. The first morning he hiked to the rear of Half-dome, a granite monolith rising vertically some three-thousand feet from the Valley floor. It had been formed over millennia by the many glaciers that had formed the Valley itself. William's map showed a trail going straight up the back of Half-dome. Reaching the point where the map showed the trail take off, William found a rough wooden ladder hugging the convex surface of the back of the dome. William stashed his pack and mounted the bottom rung of the ladder.

Ascending the ladder, William emerged above the tops of the trees growing at the rear of the dome. He suddenly felt his childhood queasiness of heights. A young man in a red jacket who had been ascending ahead of him disappeared from sight over the curvature of the stone. Pebbles dislodged by the boots of the man ahead came tumbling by William and disappearing to his rear. *Why am I doing this?*

I could get as good a view of the Valley by driving to one of the overlooks. But he was unable to stop. Rung by rung he went. The thought vaguely formed that he might keep going until driven over the edge. More bits of granite disturbed by the man ahead came tumbling by. The ladder abruptly ended. William could have easily now stood on the more gently sloping surface. But he couldn't stand. He couldn't go back. His entire body was shaking. He was bathed in cold sweat. He crawled from the ladder on his hands and knees. He saw the man in the red jacket sitting watching him from about twenty feet. The man had a broad grin. Neither spoke. William began crawling on his hands and knees until dropping to his stomach just before reaching the lip of the dome. He now inched forward until he could see Yosemite Valley three-thousand feet below. The asphalt roads appeared as mere ribbons; the cars as bugs. He was no longer being impelled forward. Every fibre of his being screamed to go back. He inched his way back until he sensed the down-slope again increasing at his feet. He felt with a foot for the top of the ladder. No ladder. *What if I'm off course from where I was in coming?* William shakily raised himself to a sitting position and looked back. The man in the red jacket was not in sight. Townsend was off his earlier course and would have missed the ladder had he kept going. He made an adjustment and resumed inching back until his right foot felt the top rung of the ladder. He started down. Ultimately he was back into the trees, and his feet finally reached the pine-needle floor. His knees buckled and he slid to the ground. Raising himself to hands and knees, he crawled to where he had stashed his pack. He lay beside it. Without intending to, he fell into a deep sleep. He awoke refreshed, prepared a mug of hot tea, and, still somewhat shaken, ate his lunch of dried fruit and cookies. He re-packed, eased his pack onto his back, and took off. He had the comfortable feeling that, although he had not overcome his fear of heights, he had functioned despite it.

* * *

Next year, William took his camping trip further south, in Sequoia National Park. Again a trauma, but less severe and different in character.

He parked and took off from Mineral King, an historic mining town in the southern Sequoia. In his first day on the trail he saw one small group of campers, then no one else. He worked his way north on the east side of the ridge on fairly gentle trails, fishing and camping as he went, then veered west to begin his ascent of the ridge. It was clear he was the first person on that particular trail that season. Small covering patches of snow were unbroken. He intended to re-cross the ridge in time to return to his car within the next three days. He planned a drive to Pasadena to visit his sister and her family—hopefully with enough trout to provide a meal or two. Stopping for his trail lunch on a granite redoubt overlooking a small stream, he saw a number of pan-sized trout holding their noses steadily into the crystal clear current. He set up his rod and selected a dry fly designed to replicate a grey mosquito—an insect that Townsend had been slapping whenever he stopped on the trail. After tying on the fly, Townsend stripped a dozen feet of line from his reel and dropped the fly in the water a bit ahead of the of trout. Woosh! A trout broke the surface to grab the fly. Townsend had an eight inch golden trout. He removed his catch and dropped the fly again a bit farther upstream. Another trout rose and took the fly. He dropped his hard-working mosquito a third time. No response. The trout were still there—at least a dozen, but they ignored the fly. The fly had served well but had worn out its welcome. Townsend went back to his tackle-bag, returned the dry fly, and took out a shiny airplane spinner. He then heated water on his Coleman burner for a second cup of tea and ate a dried pear while he sipped his tea. He realized it was running late for getting to his intended campsite on the other side of the ridge before dark, but he wanted a fresh crack at the trout. Finishing his tea, Townsend tied the spinner to his nylon line and returned to his overlook. He carefully dropped the spinner into the stream behind the group of trout and drew it up past where they were lying. Bam! One of them grabbed the spinner and was promptly lifted out of the water onto the ledge where Townsend stood. Townsend removed the hook, put the fish in his canvas creel, and returned the spinner to the stream. Another strike; another trout. Townsend again returned the spinner to the stream. No response. He could pull the spinner directly through the group of trout. None would look. Stupid they weren't.

After spending further precious minutes unsuccessfully tempting the trout with other lures, Townsend packed up and resumed his trek. The trail took him upstream. The point shown on his map for fording to the other side of the stream still had sufficient flow from the spring (now summer) runoff to prevent his crossing over without going further upstream. This took further precious minutes. He knew that in this high atmosphere when the sun went down there would be no twilight; it would suddenly become almost inky dark. He crossed the stream and continued gaining elevation on the downstream reach. He was above the timberline. There was no vegetation, but there were intermittent patches of still unmelted snow on the trail. No one had preceded him this season. He hurried. He was within perhaps three hundred yards of the ridge. If he didn't reach it quickly, he would be in shadow. Within minutes, the sun disappeared and he felt a sudden chill. He also felt a convulsion of fear. It was not that he was in any danger of falling. The trail was still clearly visible and the footing was firm, even where covered with snow. It was the utter aloneness. He knew there was no one within miles. He could have shouted his lungs out, and no one would have heard. Without his intending, his left hand went to his mouth and he found himself biting the skin around his fingernails. But he kept trudging, and within minutes reached the summit of the ridge. There was the sun, still some fifteen degrees above the horizon. His panic vanished.

24

When Herbert Brownell was appointed Attorney General in the first Eisenhower administration, he selected several Californians to his staff on recommendation of Earl Warren, including his selection of the head of the Criminal Division. When in Washington on vacation, Townsend was introduced to the head of the Criminal Division, who had worked in the Alameda County District Attorney's Office. The Assistant Attorney General invited Townsend to come to Washington to join the trial staff of the Criminal Division. Townsend accepted.

Townsend's first assignment at Justice was as one of two junior attorneys assisting a special prosecutor conduct a grand jury investigation and then a trial in federal court in St. Louis for official corruption in the White House and the Justice Department during the prior administration. The Washington team while in St. Louis was assigned space in the federal Courthouse and bunked in a downtown hotel. Although Townsend suffered some black periods when he walked deserted streets of St. Louis engulfed in fear or crouched, head in hands, in the deserted St. Louis Cathedral, he enjoyed both his work and his co-workers.

In due time, the defendants were indicted, tried before a petty jury, convicted, and sentenced to prison. The prosecutors, including Townsend, were highly commended by leading figures in the new administration and all of them were awarded promotions. More significant for Townsend, he was asked to serve as counsel to a grand jury to be convened in eastern Louisiana to investigate alleged civil rights violations that had recently received national attention. This assignment proved a watershed.

James Noe, formerly a populist governor of Louisiana in the mold of

Huey Long, had relied in part for his electoral base on blacks registered to vote in northwestern Louisiana. After the Supreme Court decision in 1954 outlawing separate-but-equal school segregation, a white citizen council movement was organized in Louisiana and other states of the deep south to resist implementation of the Supreme Court decision. The citizen councils in Louisiana soon focused on the presence of blacks on the voter registration rolls in northwest Louisiana and inaugurated a campaign to remove them. They sent teams of their members around the region to review the registration records of black voters in each parish courthouse. They did not review whites. Unsurprisingly, they consistently found defects in the records—principally misspelling or punctuation errors—indicating, in their eyes, the presence of disqualifying "illiteracy." The result of these sorties was elimination of all black voters, and no others.

Ex-governor Noe complained to the Department of Justice that the systematic purging of blacks not only discriminated against them on the basis of race in violation of the Fifteenth Amendment to the Constitution, but denied them their right as citizens of the United States to vote in federal elections. When an FBI inquiry substantiated the factual allegations, the Attorney General directed the United States Attorney to convene a federal grand jury in Monroe, Louisiana, to seek indictments under an old post Civil War statute, section 241 of title 18 of the United States Code, for conspiracy to deprive citizens of their federal right to vote for candidates for federal office, a felony. The Supreme Court had held long before, in *The Civil Rights Cases*, that section 241 did not apply to discrimination on the basis of race in violation of the Fourteenth or Fifteenth Amendments, but that it did apply to conspiracy to deprive a citizen of the United States of any right that particularly inhered in his status as a U.S. citizen, such as his right to travel in interstate commerce, his right to petition Congress, his right to federal protection while in federal custody, his right to contract with the federal government, and his right to serve in the U.S. military. His right to vote for candidates for federal office was such a right.

On recommendation of the Assistant Attorney General in charge of the Criminal Division, the Attorney General directed the United States

Attorney for the Western District of Louisiana, headquartered in Shreveport, to request the U.S. District Court to convene a federal grand jury in Monroe to investigate possible violations of 18 U.S.C. 241 within the Eastern Division of the District. The Court ordered the grand jury convened, and the U.S. Attorney requested the Assistant Attorney General to assign a trial attorney from Washington to assist in the inquiry. The Assistant Attorney General promptly assigned Townsend.

Townsend flew to Shreveport, where he spent a day acquainting himself with the office and the files and meeting with the two FBI agents who had been directing the investigation. He then flew on to Monroe with the U.S. Attorney, who would introduce him to the grand jury. The grand jury, comprising twenty-three members, had been specially empaneled from the voter rolls maintained by the parish clerk in each parish courthouse within the Division. All of the jurors were white. Two of them were women, one a farm wife and the other a college-educated business woman. The twenty-one men were drawn approximately half from the country-side and half from town.

The first day was consumed with introductions, with the U.S. Attorney's explanation of the Grand Jury's role, and with Townsend's explanation of 18 U.S.C. 241. Thanks to extensive news coverage, the jurors already knew why they were there. The U.S. Attorney lectured them that the law precluded their revealing anything occurring in the in the grand jury room.

"The law forbids any of you or any of us lawyers from the disclosing any of the proceedings before the grand jury. On the other hand, a witness is free to disclose what happened during his own appearance. Thus a witness may disclose what questions he was asked and what answers he gave.

"Mr. Townsend has been designated by the Attorney General of the United States to assist you in your inquiry. He will issue subpoenas for witnesses to appear before you and will question the witnesses in your presence. Each of you will be free to ask additional questions.

"When Mr. Townsend believes the facts have been sufficiently inquired into, he may submit to you proposed indictments for your vote. You should arrange to spend about three weeks working on this grand jury.

"I will now retire while you select a foreman to preside over your proceedings. Mr. Townsend will call your first witness Monday morning at 9:00 o'clock"

* * *

The first witness that Townsend called was the registrar of voters for one of the parishes. The registrar had described to the FBI how a group of eight members of the local White Citizens' Council had come to his office one morning and asked access to the voting registration cards, which are public records. He lead them to the files and they started through them, file by file. They took out and laid aside all cards indicated as for black voters and stacked them for further review next day.

Next morning they returned, divided among them the cards they had set aside, and reviewed each card. The registrar noted that the men had made red checks, mostly by spelling or punctuation errors. They returned the cards to the registrar and filled out a card for each one challenging the legality of the registration. When the registrar had all of the cards, he mailed each of the challenged voters a notice that he had been purged from the roles because he was not qualified. He was told that if he disagreed, he could file suit in the parish circuit court. No white voters were challenged or disqualified. No blacks went unchallenged.

The next day, the challenging members of the White Citizens' were called before the grand jury. Townsend anticipated that at least some would claim the protection of the Fifth Amendment and refuse to testify. On the other hand, some had consented to interview by the FBI and would likely answer questions to the grand jury. They could be expected to say that they were simply exercising their rights under Louisiana law and the voters they chose to challenge were all illegally registered. They were properly removed from the roles.

After questioning the white challengers, Townsend called before the grand jury a number of well-educated black voters who had told Townsend that they had been voting regularly until receiving their notice of disqualification. They had not sought review of their removal because they thought it useless.

Townsend repeated this process for the other six parishes that had been the subject of FBI investigation.

When the testimony was concluded, Townsend, with the United States Attorney seated beside him, explained the applicable law.

"Section 241 of title 18 of the United States Code has provided since 1866 that if two or more persons conspire to deprive a citizen of the United States of any right under the Constitution or laws of the United States, they shall be punished as there provided. One of the rights we have as citizens is the right to vote for candidates for federal office, including the offices of United States congressman, senator, and presidential elector. In Louisiana, a prerequisite for voting for those offices is registration with the parish registrar of voters. Thus, a conspiracy to unlawfully prevent a citizen from registering or maintaining his registration as a voter with the registrar would violate section 241.

"Here, the question for you is whether there is probable cause to believe that two or more of the individuals who challenged the citizens removed from the voting rolls agreed to do so for reasons other than legitimate concern for their qualifications as voters, and if one or more of the removed voters were in fact qualified, then the challengers were engaged in a conspiracy to deprive the challenged voters of their rights under the laws of the United States."

The grand jury deliberated for three hours but returned no indictments.

25

Townsend was neither surprised nor dismayed by the grand jury's failure to indict. It was clear that the jurors had seriously considered the government's evidence and Townsend suspected that there had even been some votes for indicting. At least, he was sure the jurors had accepted the legitimacy of the federal interest. He also knew that the White Citizen Council members had not been comfortable in their grand jury appearances and would not soon repeat what they must now see to have been conduct with which many grand jurors were unsympathetic. Townsend knew that the Justice Department had followed the right course, and he was comfortable with his own role.

But basic change would come slowly. When Townsend went out the heavy swinging doors of the courthouse one day in Monroe he was walking with two FBI agents he had worked with throughout the case. They held the doors for Townsend. He, in turn, held one door for the next person through. It happened to be a black woman and a small girl, likely her daughter.

The woman thanked him for holding the door.

"How about stopping for a cup of coffee?"

After they were served, one agent spoke.

"You've been doing great down here, but it's the little things that do you in. Like holding the door for the black lady back at the courthouse. Everybody seeing you knew that you were from the north. Not necessary."

"But I can't change a lifetime of habit. And I can't believe it's necessary. More than that, I think it was a nice thing to do."

"No doubt it was. Just trying to smooth your way."

"Thanks."

Given the cultural rift, it was clear to Townsend that juries would not function to determine racial discrimination. The law required a more sure means where basic civil rights, such as the right to vote, were involved.

A year or so earlier, Townsend had been involved in a lawsuit brought in the name of the United States against Governor Orville Faubus of Arkansas to enjoin his interference in the desegregation of Central High School in Little Rock pursuant to a court order entered in a suit brought by the NAACP. When the Governor, for the stated reason of maintaining public order, ordered his national guard to block nine black students from entering the school pursuant a federal court order, President Eisenhower reacted quickly and firmly. Although he had doubted the wisdom of the Supreme Court's decision in the Brown case, he had no doubt of his own responsibility when a state governor used his national guard to frustrate the order of a federal court. He ordered the Arkansas guard into federal service, countermanded the governor's order, and directed federal troops to the scene to provide necessary protection to the students. At the same time, the federal judge specially assigned from another district directed the attorney general to appear in the school desegregation case as *amicus* to take such action as might be appropriate to protect the integrity of the federal court. The appropriate legal action was a civil suit to enjoin the Governor from illegally interfering with the execution of a federal court order. But there was no federal statute authorizing such a suit by the Attorney General. No matter, such authority was implied from the very existence of the federal government. How could the chief legal officer of the nation *not* have authority to seek court relief when the functioning of the nation's courts was illegally obstructed? And the same question could be asked about illegal obstruction to voting in national elections. How could the chief legal officer of the nation *not* have access to the courts to remove such obstruction?

At any rate, Townsend and the Assistant Attorney General in charge of his division thought such an argument was worth a shot, and the Assistant Attorney General directed Townsend to prepare a lawsuit and a memorandum of justification for the Attorney General in the Lousiana voting matter.

The Attorney General convened a meeting of his top assistants to consider the proposed suit. Townsend was later told their view was unanimous—the suit should not be filed. They saw no lack of merit to the suit itself but felt it politically inappropriate at that time. The administration was just then considering an omnibus civil right bill which would include authorization for the type of suit by the attorney general that Townsend was proposing. Be that as it may, Townsend was very disappointed that the Attorney General would not proceed without waiting for legislation. It would be some years before Townsend accepted the wisdom of that decision. In any event the Civil Rights Act of 1957 was eventually enacted including the provision for voting right suits by the attorney general.

* * *

The attention of the Attorney General was next directed, on civil rights, to the beautiful strip of white sand running along the Gulf Coast past Biloxi, Mississippi. The national press, with appropriate photos, had reported that denizens of local pool halls, using baseball bats, pool cues, 2x4s, tire-irons, and anything else handy, had assaulted a group of blacks, including women and children, who were peacefully seeking to picnic and bathe at the beach in front of Biloxi. The press reported that the local NAACP had informed local law enforcement, both police and sheriff's office, in advance of the intended picnic. No law enforcement officer was at the scene. There were no arrests. When interviewed, local officials said they understood the beach was privately owned by landowners whose property fronted on the beach. The news reports mentioned that the white sand for the beach had been dredged from the Gulf under a contract with the U.S. Army Corps of Engineers.

The Civil Rights Division obtained a copy of the contract the Corp of Engineers had signed with Harrison County, Mississippi, for construction of the beach. It bound the county to maintain the beach, once constructed, for "public use." The Attorney General wrote the Secretary of the Army noting the press reports and stating his view that the County's promise to maintain the beach for public use included a commitment to maintain law and order so that the entire public could use the beach without racial discrimination. The Corp of Engineers relayed this advice to Harrison County. The County responded that the beach was private property and beyond its control. Thereupon, the Civil Rights Division prepared and the Attorney General filed a civil action against Harrison County in the name of the United States in federal court in Gulfport, Mississippi.

William Townsend had been assigned preparation of the beach case and was now assigned as trial attorney, assisted by another attorney from Civil Rights Division and an attorney from Lands Division.

Harrison County filed a motion to dismiss the lawsuit upon the ground of failure to join indispensable defendants—namely, some eighteen hundred or so owners of property abutting the beach. The United States opposed the motion on the ground that the private owners had no legal interest in the area of the beach because it lay beyond the line of mean high tide existing prior to its construction by dredging under the contract with the Corp of Engineers. Asserting the land title question to be an issue of Mississippi law, the County argued that the State Supreme Court had determined that the title was held by the abutting owners. The federal judge, a courtly old gentleman and long-time incumbent on the bench, granted the County's motion to dismiss but allowed the United States thirty days within which to add the beach front owners as party defendants. Rather than go through a preliminary round of appellate litigation, the federal team decided to add the parties as directed. Service of summons on the over one thousand new defendants changed both the character and atmosphere of the suit. It became a moderately well organized circus. Every law firm with an office in the county and many from elsewhere packed the courtroom at every public setting. Simply calling the case and getting a response from those present took over an hour.

The landowners separately moved to dismiss on the ground that they were not parties to the contract with the Corp of Engineers, that the accretion to the beach in front of their properties belonged to them, and that there was no allegation that they had consented to the use of their beach front by the picnickers. The federal prosecutors decided it could be useful if they were prepared to prove that the parking bays located every hundred yards or so on the beach side of U.S. 90 were regularly used by the public and that some evidence of this would be the nature and volume of the trash deposited daily in the large wire-mesh containers at each bay. Thus, the origin of the "trash detail."

"I agree that we need a trash detail, but I do *not* agree to my designation as detailee. This has got to be a Lands Division function and a Lands Division attorney can follow the trash all the way to the landfill. In any event, Frank already has the trashiest room and will be least discommoded by a bit more. I'm ready for a vote."

"Wait a minute. Since when have strategic decisions in this case been made by majority vote? If we can't agree on something fundamental to the case, we go up the line. I'm willing to take this to my assistant AG. If you two want to go to yours, maybe it will even go on up the attorney general."

"Fine. Maybe he'll resolve it by offering to keep the trash, properly labeled, in his office. He certainly has room for it, and he could have the FBI deliver it."

"Knowing the Director, that might require a presidential order. And even an order might not get it done. Might require a constitutional amendment."

Levity aside, the federal team finally settled on asking the FBI to check the trash cans once a day, determine the general nature of the contents, and take a photo. The agents did this without checking with headquarters. As it developed, direct evidence of the trash was not needed on the trial. In pretrial the County conceded that it maintained both the bays and the trash containers for the general public.

After a two week trial, the Court ruled that the beach was privately owned and dismissed the government's case. The government appealed, the judgment was reversed, and the County was enjoined from failing to maintain law and order on the beach. The beach was thereafter used by blacks without incident.

26

The first case under the Civil Rights Act of 1957 to remedy denial of the right to vote arose in Terrell County, Georgia, a rural county where blacks had for years been denied registration to vote on the pretext they were not literate in English. The FBI was directed to conduct a full investigation, which confirmed the details of the complaint. The local chapter of the NAACP had promoted a campaign to encourage blacks to apply for registration. It had conducted workshops to familiarize blacks with the forms and procedures, and to practice a "literacy" test they would be facing. Selecting a dozen or so of those appearing best qualified, the NAACP took them to the registrar's office at 9:30 on a bright sunny morning. They hit a stone wall. A wall covered with velvet, but of stone nonetheless.

The registrar was the scion of an old Terrell County family who had taken the job as a public service. He was soft-spoken, polite to all, and diligent in his duties. He was well-read and widely traveled. He personally handled all applications by blacks, while his deputies generally handled whites. He believed that all legally qualified individuals were entitled to vote and should do so. He believed he had never discriminated against a black and would not permit his staff to do so. On the other hand, he believed that all legal requirements for voting, including the requirement of English literacy, should be enforced.

As part of the Department's investigation, the Civil Rights Division asked the FBI to obtain and bring to Washington copies of all records of the Terrell County Registrar. A systematic review disclosed that *all* applications marked with an "*n*" had been denied; all marked "*w*" had been approved. It also disclosed many of the "*n*" applications were in excellent handwriting, while some of the "*w*" applications were hardly legible. Townsend suggested the Department subpoena a representative number of white applicants with the worst handwriting to test their literacy on the record and under oath. The assigned trial attorney disagreed. In his view, doing so would serve only to embarrass the white applicants while producing no evidence probative in the case. The illiteracy of registered whites had no bearing, he argued, on the literacy of blacks. If Townsend insisted on deposing whites, the assigned trial attorney would ask to withdraw from active participation in the case. Townsend did insist; the trial attorney did withdraw, and Townsend was asked to take over.

* * *

The depositions of the white applicants for registration were taken in the Terrell County Courthouse, a large barn of a building that apparently served as a multi-purpose meeting hall. It had large double doors in front, a vestibule, a raised podium in front of an illuminated "Drink Coca Cola" electric clock, plank walls, a linoleum floor, and a speaker system. Apart from the witnesses, who were subpoenaed to appear at half-hour intervals, the depositions were attended by the court reporter, the registrar/defendant, his lawyer from Atlanta, and the assigned (although now inactive) lawyer from the Justice Department, who would be handling the government's documents. After preliminary questions eliciting the witness's name, address, age and occupation, Townsend proceeded with his direct examination.

"Do you recognize this document?"

"Yes, suh. That is my application to register as a voter."

"Is that your writing?"

"Yes, suh. I filled it out in the Registrar's Office."

"Did the registrar ask you to read aloud a short passage from the Constitution of the United States?"

"Yes, he sure did."

"Did you read it?"

"Yes, I sure did. He said I read it fine and that I would receive a notice in the mail."

"Did you receive a notice?"

"Yes, I received notice that I was registered."

"I would like to show you this slip of paper on which I have typed some language from Article I, paragraph 9 of the Constitution of the United States. Have you seen this language before?"

"I think so. I think that's what the registrar asked me to read out loud."

"Will you please read it out loud for me now? Take your time."

"Of course. 'No...State...shall...'"

The witness stopped and looked up.

"Go ahead."

"I can't quite make out the next word."

"That will be all. Thank you."

* * *

When the case came to trial, Townsend called as the government's first witnesses a number of rejected black applicants.

"What is your full name?"

"Henry Caleb Oates."

"Where do you live?"

"819 Stuart Street, Dawson, Georgia."

"How long have you lived there?"

"Fourteen and a half years."

"Do you have family living with you?"

"Yes. My wife, my mother, and my three children—two boys, of three years and five years, and a girl of nine years."

"How are you employed?"

"I am a teacher at the Booker T. Washington High School."

"Are you registered to vote?"

"No. I applied to register, but was turned down."

"When did you apply?"

"First time, about four years ago. I have applied three times."

"Please describe the last time."

"It was last December, in the week before Christmas. I went to the Registrar's Office in the morning with my neighbor, Tim Jones. The Registrar was sitting behind his desk reading a newspaper. He got up, said good morning, shook hands, and asked what he could do for us. We said we would like to register to vote. He said fine and gave each of us a printed application. He said that when we had completed the forms he would administer the English literacy test. Mr. Jones and I completed our forms and handed them back to the Registrar. I don't think he looked at the forms, but he may have. In any event, he put them on his desk and brought back a slip of paper with a short sentence typed on it. He handed it to me and asked me to read the sentence out loud. I read it to him and handed it back. He did the same thing with Tim."

"I would like to show you this printed card that I have marked 'Deposition Ex.1.' Do you recognize this card?"

"Yes. That's the application card that the Registrar gave me."

"Was it filled in when he gave it to you?"

"No, I filled it in, and then gave it back. These red check marks, though, are his."

"Did you write the word 'bilogy' next to this red check?"

"I'm embarrassed to say I did. I meant 'biology'."

"Did anyone call your attention to your error?"

"No, sir."

"Do you know how to spell 'biology.'?"

"Yes, sir. I teach biology in high school."

"I would like to show you a slip of paper that I have marked 'Deposition Ex. 2.' Do you recognize that?"

"Yes, that's the slip of paper the Registrar asked me to read."

"Please read out loud what it says."

"'No State shall lay any imposts or duties on imports or exports.'"

"Then what happened?"

"I handed this slip back to him, and he said we would hear from him. I got a written notice after New Years saying my application for registration to vote had been denied."

And so it went. Townsend called a number of rejected black applicants for registration with substantially the same results. They all had at least a high school education and some had attended college. All read handily the constitutional provision used by the Registrar. Townsend then turned to the white registered voters.

"Your honor, we propose now to demonstrate the level of literacy that the defendant requires of white applicants for voter registration. We will do this through the defendant's official records and through depositions taken from a number of white registered voters. I am sensitive to the general rule that a deposition may not used in lieu of live testimony unless the witness cannot be subpoenaed. Here, however, it is not *testimony* that is sought, but rather a *demonstration.* If the height of an individual was a fact in controversy, I assume a party could subpoena the individual for a measurement. No less, where literacy is in issue we should be able to introduce demonstrative evidence even if it is coincidentally in a deposition. Since the evidence is more graphic in live rendition, we ask that the court admit the recording of the deposition, rather than a transcription."

"Any objection? Very well, you may proceed."

Townsend called the court reporter who had taken the depositions. The reporter set up his equipment and commenced playing the tape of the first deposition. When he reached the point at which the witness was asked to read the constitutional directive that "No State shall...*lay* any imposts or duties on imports or exports," and the witness stopped reading after the word "shall," a raspy stage whisper could clearly be heard from the recording, "lay, *lay*, like an egg."

Townsend had not previously listened to the recording of the deposition, and had not realized that these words had been recorded. The Judge interceded.

"Whose voice was that?" he asked the stenographic reporter.

"That was defense counsel, seated on the other side of the witness."

"Very well, proceed."

The rest of the recording confirmed that the white voter was unable to read "lay." Depositions of other white voters displayed similar reading problems. All of the offered deposition recordings were admitted in evidence.

In due course, judgment was entered for the government and a permanent injunction issued requiring the defendant to register as voters the black applicants who had applied and restraining him from discriminating against blacks in the future.

The State of Georgia appealed the judgment to the United States Supreme Court, arguing that the Civil Rights Act unconstitutionally intruded upon state authority, and that the record here in any event failed to establish discrimination. The Supreme Court unanimously affirmed.

27

If William Townsend had given it any thought, he would have realized he had reached full maturation as a litigating attorney in the years since receiving his law degree. Although he had approached his career with something akin to terror, he had successfully navigated a full range of confrontational settings—court trials, jury trials, appeals, grand jury proceedings. But a different sort of contested proceeding was about to appear on his horizon—a full-blown administrative proceeding.

The summer of 1961 brought the *Freedom Rides.* Increasing enrolment of black students in traditionally unsegregated institutions of higher education outside the South, a new infusion of students enjoying the benefits of the GI bill, and perhaps a new impatience by ex-service members to discrimination, brought new activism to the civil rights scene. Whatever the reasons for the timing, public bus transportation presented itself as an almost irresistible target for public protest during spring break and summer vacation. And the protests fed on themselves and upon any counter-demonstrations. Law enforcement officials in the deep south used increasing force in suppressing demonstrations. Fire-hoses and police dogs were enlisted. The administration decided to seek broad relief against interstate carriers in an administrative proceeding before the Interstate Commerce Commission. Townsend was assigned the task of supervising preparation of the proceeding and ultimately of presenting the government's case to the full Commission.

The Department had received from the public in the preceding three years 39 complaints from seventeen southern and border states of racial discrimination in interstate bus terminals and buses. It now requested the FBI to observe the terminal facilities in the cities in each of those states in which the Bureau maintained an office. The survey identified 97 terminals in or on which signs were posted indicating use by one or the other race. The Bureau was instructed to take photographs, which were assembled in an appendix to the government's brief before the Commission. Another appendix tabulated individual citizen complaints of discrimination.

The Motor Carriers Act had long forbidden discrimination by interstate bus carriers and it had more recently held the prohibition extended to segregation by race. The Commission, however, although having had the authority to do so, had never by general rule stated the prohibition against racial segregation on buses and in terminals. But if the case was properly made asking the Commission to publish a regulation, it should be like shooting fish in a barrel. Nonetheless, Townsend felt a knot of apprehension in his stomach—something he had gradually lost in court proceedings over the years.

The Commission hearing went well. The entire membership of the Commission sat for the oral argument, and there were no surprises. It promptly promulgated a regulation that included everything the government requested. Both the assistant attorney general in charge of the Civil Rights Division and his first assistant thought that William had performed well. William had fully matured as a professional litigator. But there were other aspects of his life in which fear pervaded.

28

Townsend knew that his mother did not fear the thought of her personal mortality. In his last visit to her, while she was living with total care, he sat next to her bed while she reminisced.

"We can't really know what comes after our death."

"No, I don't think we can."

"I simply think of your dad. If it was good enough for him, it's good enough for me."

A few years earlier, while Townsend's mother was still active but after his father's death, his mother underwent a remarkable physical transformation. Through much of her life she had suffered very painful arthritis. It defied treatment and was greatly aggravated by physical activity, most notably gardening. After struggling for years, she finally gave up gardening completely. That was until the arthritis inexplicably diminished and finally disappeared. She resumed gardening. Townsend conjectured that she had resolved some inner tension that underlay the arthritis.

29

As Townsend gained confidence in his professional life, he found himself with increased stirring of sexuality. It started while he was still in law school.

For his last two years of law school, Townsend lived in International House, where he had a private room on one of the men's floors. From time to time he noticed a particularly lovely Norwegian girl. She had a long blond braid, a willowy figure, and eyes of the deepest blue he had ever seen. Occasionally they sat at the same dining room table without speaking to each other. He learned, willy-nilly, that she was a psychology major.

Townsend worked daily in the dining hall, either on the cafeteria line or on the dishwasher. He had noticed that the Norwegian girl worked on the line. One day when the work staff were all standing in the kitchen waiting for some program to finish in the dining hall, the Norwegian girl walked up to him and spoke.

"My name is Ingrid. What is your name?"

"My name is Melbourne." William was unsure why he was using his middle name.

"Milberg?"

"No, Melbourne—M, E, L, B, O, U, R, N, E—Melbourne," said Townsend with a slight smile.

The girl, flustered, looked down and stepped away without either of them saying more.

A few weeks later, Townsend was walking up Bancroft Avenue carrying a very large hat box containing a straw hat Townsend intended to give his mother for Easter. Ingrid, coming from his rear, fell into step with him.

"Who is the hat for?"

"My mother. She loves hats."

The two walked to the door of International House side by side without speaking. At the door, Ingrid opened it for Townsend to go through with his box.

One day Townsend was seated at lunch opposite a student he occasionally sat and visited with. Ingrid came with her lunch tray and sat next to the student. The student mentioned that he visited a house of assignation about once a month. When Townsend mildly remonstrated, the student responded, "I don't have a choice. If I didn't go every month, I would die."

"See, you do have a choice."

Every time Townsend saw Ingrid, even at a distance, it was a notable event in his life. On the last day the dining hall was open after Townsend had successfully completed his third year of law school, Townsend was seated at his lunch when Ingrid came sailing in and plunked down across the table. Townsend's stomach began churning.

"What do you do now that you've graduated?"

"Go home and study for the bar exam."

"And then?"

"If I pass, I have to find a job."

"Where?"

"Somewhere in the Bay Area. I don't know just where."

"You won't go back to your home town?"

"No. My mother will want me to, but I want to get away."

Townsend did not ask Ingrid what her plans were. He left the table with a simple goodby.

* * *

We have already seen how Townsend organized his time, studied, and passed the bar exam after graduation from law school. We have not seen how his memory of Ingrid persisted. Despite concentration on his studies, the thought of Ingrid kept intruding. Finally, with the bar exam in San Francisco on the horizon, he decided he would try to contact her. He wrote a postcard to her at International House. He said simply that he would be in San Francisco in the near future and hoped to see her.

Would she let him know how to contact her? No response. He called International House, but they would not release a forwarding address. He was blocked for now.

When Townsend commenced working for the Alameda County District Attorney in Oakland, he continued living in Berkeley. He also dropped in at International House with the hope of picking up some clue to Ingrid's whereabouts.

"We can't give out forwarding addresses. Address a letter here and we will forward it for you."

"But I need to deliver a package of perishables."

"Oh, alright. She lives nearby. Let me dig out her address card."

The clerk produced a Ingrid's card with an address for an apartment in Berkeley. Townsend walked the four blocks to the apartment building and walked the three floors up to her apartment. When he knocked, the door was opened by Ingrid. She recognized Townsend and invited him in.

The apartment was in some disarray, with both men's and women's clothes strewn about and dirty dishes in the sink. The door to a back bedroom was open, and a young man, fully clothed, was sitting with his feet, shoes on, up on the bed, reviewing a typewritten manuscript.

"Won't you sit down?"

"Thanks. I just wanted to learn if you knew anything about what had happened to Henry or Sadar," former residents of International House whom Ingrid and Townsend had known.

Ingrid and Townsend chatted a bit about old times and he then excused himself. She did not introduce the man in the bedroom.

30

In both Berkeley and Washington, D.C., Townsend had continued his practice, first established in high school, of enlisting a female date when the social context seemed to call for one. But he had no regular or serious girl friend. This changed as the result of an airplane ride to Boston.

Townsend had been invited by his boss's secretary at the Justice Department, with whom he occasionally played tennis, to spend a long weekend with her and her parents at their summer home in Kennebunkport, Maine. On the Boston leg of his trip, he sat on the airplane next to a young lady with whom he almost immediately struck up a conversation. She worked for a travel agency in Washington and was going to Boston to visit her parents. The two of them chattered the entire way, hugely enjoying each other's company. Townsend asked for and she gave him her telephone number in Washington.

Back in Washington the following week, Townsend called his Boston flight companion, Barbara, and invited her to lunch. At lunch, they picked up where they had left off on the flight. More lunches followed. When Townsend had out-of-town visitors from California, Barbara joined them for lunch. They began weekend lunches at each other's apartments. William shared a large apartment with two other bachelor lawyers from the Justice Department. Barbara shared a much smaller apartment with her sister and a girl friend.

One weekend when Townsend's room mates were out of town, Barbara and William were watching the Wimbledon matches on the TV in Townsend's apartment. They sat next to each other on the sofa facing the set. When their hands inadvertently touched, William took and kissed her hand. She leaned into him, and he began exploring her body with his other hand. With her help, he began removing her clothing. With her clothing removed, she began removing his. When they were fully disrobed, William drew Barbara to her feet, picked her up in his arms, and walked to his bedroom. She was light as a feather.

He laid Barbara on his bed and lay beside her. Neither spoke. She reached across and lightly put her right hand on his chest. She moved it down and began gently stroking his stomach. Thoroughly aroused, he mounted her. While he was raised on his elbows on either side of her head, she grasped his upper arms and began gently guiding his body forward and back an inch or so on her body. With her guidance, he began rhythmically moving forward and back with her legs locked around his. Forward and back. Forward and back. He suddenly and emphatically ejaculated. Gasping, he rolled off onto his back. They lay panting, not speaking. After some minutes, Barbara sat up, leaned over, and lightly kissed William's limp penis.

William rose, went into the bathroom, and returned with a wet cloth and a dry towel. He cleaned her and then himself. He lay again with neither speaking.

They heard a sudden rattling at the front door of the apartment. William rose and hurriedly put his undershorts. As he entered the living room, the front door opened. It was the cleaning lady. *Why in the world would she be coming on a Saturday?*

"Would you mind coming back a bit later? It's inconvenient right now."

"Of course."

"Maybe in an hour?"

When Barbara and William left the apartment he was relieved that they did not see the cleaning lady in the outside hall.

As William drove Barbara to her home, she spoke obliquely of what they had experienced. She said she considered her job to be giving a man confidence. She said that her roommate had told her that she and her boyfriend had gone to sleep one night joined to each other. They awoke the next morning still joined, and when she moved a bit he stiffened and they had another mutual orgasm. William felt the old knot of fear forming in his stomach. Things were moving faster than he could handle.

William parked his car in front of Barbara's apartment house and saw her to the door. She unlocked and opened the door.

William said, "Thanks for joining me for the Wimbledon."

"Don't thank me. When will I see you again?"

"I'll give you a call."

"You're still planning lunch with my parents and me next Wednesday?"

"Yes, I'll see you at the Hay-Adams at noon."

Next Wednesday, William was the first to arrive at the Hay-Adams. Barbara arrived with her parents, her sister and her sister's boy-friend. Her mother was a handsome woman, fashionably dressed and with an almost regal bearing. Her father was a pleasant looking fellow, somewhat shorter than his wife, with a full head of greying hair. Mother carried the burden of conversation.

"We're glad to be finally meeting you. Barbara has told us something of your work, and we're hoping to hear more. Perhaps we can see you sometime in Boston."

Barbara's father spoke sparingly. Townsend already knew that he was head chef in one of Boston's fanciest restaurants. Townsend had assumed, without being told, that her parents had first met when he was catering some function at her home.

Lunch conversation was sprightly, with everyone joining. At one point, when it lagged a bit, Barbara looked across at her mother.

"Well, what do you think of him?"

Her mother, looking directly at William, said, "I like him, but I think he's a bit silly."

No one spoke. William looked at his hands in his lap.

"That's true. I am silly."

Again no one spoke until Barbara's mother asked something about the Cherry Blossom Festival. William was able to answer and did so. Conversation again took off.

When they broke from lunch, William and Barbara's mother shared a taxi. He held the door for her and she plunked down in the center of the back seat. When he got in, he had to squeeze a bit. Once underway, Barbara's mother leaned in to William whenever they made a left turn. William knew she was sending him a message, but he was unsure what it was. Whatever, it was positive.

31

Barbara and William continued having occasional lunches together downtown, but did not lunch again in each other's apartments. They still very much enjoyed each other's company, but she seemed to have touched something that lead him to draw away.

As a general matter, Townsend's interest in the opposite sex continued to increase with his increasing confidence in his professional role. In his fifth year in Washington, D.C., he met at a small dinner party a young lady, some eight years his junior, who had come to Washington as an *au perre* with her aunt and her aunt's husband on his re-assignment in the U.S. foreign service. The guests of honor at the dinner, who were friends of Townsend from California, had connived for Townsend to drive the young lady home after the dinner. In the drive home, he invited her to join him in visiting the National Gallery of Art and having lunch the next day with his California friends. Next day's outing went swimmingly. When she returned to her aunt and uncle's home after the lunch, her aunt asked how it had gone.

"I have just had lunch with the man I am going to marry."

"You silly goose. You know no such thing."

Her aunt proved wrong. Maria proved right.

Townsend and Maria began dating regularly. When Maria's aunt and uncle took their two children vacationing on the eastern shore, they invited Townsend to come down and visit at their cabin on weekends. While he was there, Townsend and Maria slept at opposite ends of a long screen porch. On two occasions, after all others had gone to bed, Maria came to Townsend's bed. Thus began a series of encounters culminating in her pregnancy.

"Do your aunt and uncle know?"

"No, but I will tell them. I will have to tell them, because I intend to go ahead and have the baby."

"We will get married."

In the months leading to the pregnancy, Townsend well knew of the possibility. He was indulging in unguarded sex but was strangely indifferent to the consequences. He was comfortable in letting them play out as they might. In the three years while taking phenobarbital after his *gran mal* seizure at age nineteen he had ceased having wet dreams and had wondered if he was sterile. Now he knew.

Thus, Townsend started down a new road. At some level, he knew that he had backed into marriage; he had not come to it straight on. And he was terrified. But he thought he understood the course on which he was set and was resolved to see it through.

Printed in the United States
64889LVS00003B/369